Travels in Alsace & Lorraine

Ribeauvillé

Travels in
Alsace & Lorraine

Mary Elsy
with
Jill Norman

MEREHURST PRESS
LONDON

Published 1989 by Merehurst Press
Ferry House, 51-57 Lacy Road,
Putney, London SW15 1PR

Co-Published in Australia and New Zealand by
Child and Associates
5 Skyline Place, French's Forest
Sydney 2086
Australia

ISBN 1 85391 040 6

Designed and produced by Snap! Books

Printed in Great Britain by Butler and Tanner Ltd,
Frome, Somerset

Typeset by Maggie Spooner Typesetting
Illustrations by Ann Johns
Maps by Sue Lawes
Cover illustration: A canal at Strasbourg by Charles
Pyne. By kind permission of Victoria and Albert
Museum/Bridgeman Art Library.

Contents

Duroc Square, Pont-à-Mousson

Author's Preface

Both Alsace and Lorraine have much to offer the tourist. Alsace especially, situated at a main European crossroads, is easily accessible. Strasbourg, home of Europe's parliament, and Colmar, are two of France's most beautiful and civilised cities. You can climb the Vosges' northern peaks or follow the well-marked wine roads, passing vineyards and sleepy flower-decked, picture-postcard villages and towns. Then there's the food! Alsatians, bon vivants, are big eaters and their region is noted for its distinctive Franco-German cuisine — black puddings, foie gras, sauerkraut and fruit tarts — all washed-down with light, cool, fruity Alsatian wines.

Lorraine boasts Nancy and Metz, two proud prominent historic capitals: also Vittel and Contrexéville, two celebrated spas. Lorraine, noted for its quiche, castles, churches and glassware, was the site of many famous European battles. It was also the birthplace of Joan of Arc, France's greatest heroine. The heavy industries, now in decline, are mainly concentrated in the north. Southwards lie rolling farmlands, woods, lakes and orchards, which undulate gently towards and merge into the leafy Vosges range, an ideal countryside for walkers.

The central part of *Travels in Alsace & Lorraine* provides a plan for a 13-days' tour of Alsace and Lorraine, beginning at Strasbourg. Then from the heights of the northern Vosges it traverses the region through the wine roads to Colmar and ascends via Munster and Col de la Schlucht to the Route des Crêtes. After exploring this area, head next to Gérardmer, then Lorraine's famous spas and, if time, the southern end of the Route des Crêtes, passing the Vosges' highest peaks. Nancy, Toul, Joan of Arc country, the battlefields of Verdun, and Metz, complete the tour.

The itinerary provides a basic route for each day and for those with time available, offers suggestions for additional trips marked within the text as *Detours*.

To give added interest to your journey the following section offers background information on aspects of the region — most particularly its cuisine. The final section gives some sample menus and recipes of the region's most typical dishes.

Joan of Arc's birthplace,
Domrémy-la-Pucelle

Introduction
to
Alsace and Lorraine

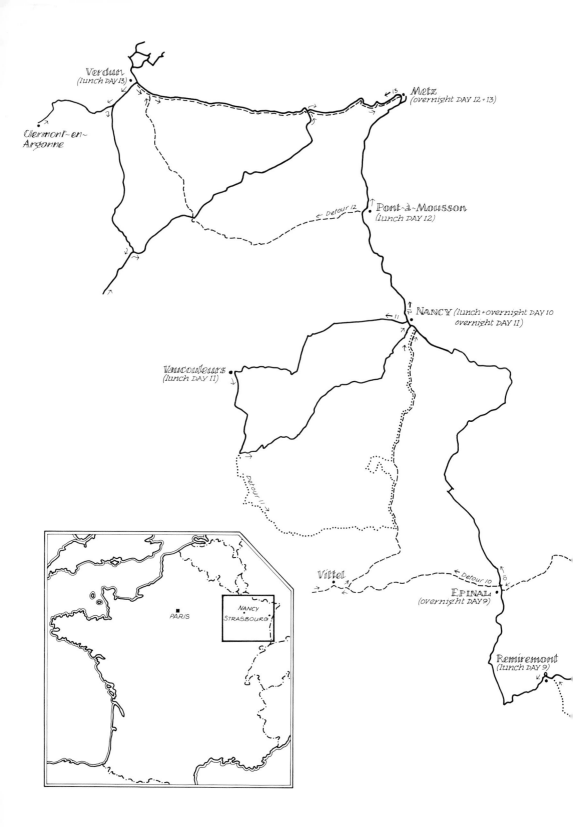

Verdun
(lunch DAY 13)

Clermont-en-
Argonne

Metz
(overnight DAY 12 + 13)

13

Detour 12

Pont-à-Mousson
(lunch DAY 12)

NANCY (lunch + overnight DAY 10
overnight DAY 11)

11

Vaucouleurs
(lunch DAY 11)

Detour 11

Vittel

Detour 10

10

EPINAL
(overnight DAY 9)

Remiremont
(lunch DAY 9)

PARIS

NANCY
STRASBOURG

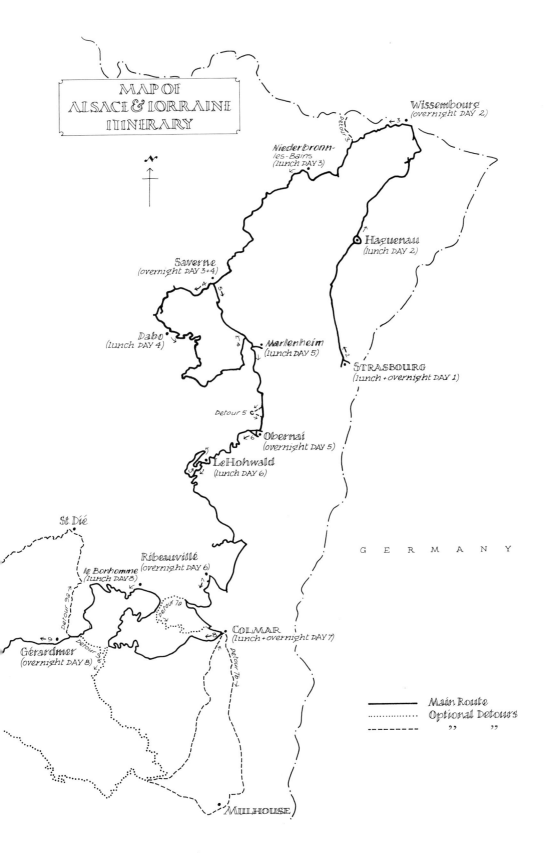

MAP OF
ALSACE & LORRAINE
ITINERARY

Wissembourg
(overnight DAY 2)

Detour 3

Niederbronn-
les-Bains
(lunch DAY 3)

Haguenau
(lunch DAY 2)

Saverne
(overnight DAY 3+4)

Dabo
(lunch DAY 4)

Marlenheim
(lunch DAY 5)

STRASBOURG
(lunch + overnight DAY 1)

Detour 5

Obernai
(overnight DAY 5)

LeHohwald
(lunch DAY 6)

St Dié

GERMANY

Ribeauvillé
(overnight DAY 6)

le Bonhomme
(lunch DAY 8)

Detour 9a

Detour 7a

Detour 9b

COLMAR
(lunch + overnight DAY 7)

Gérardmer
(overnight DAY 8)

Detour 7b

Main Route
Optional Detours
"   "

MULHOUSE

Colmar

Land Use and Agriculture

A motorist driving through Alsace, Vosges and Lorraine will pass through a variety of scenery.

Alsace's plains stretch to the Rhine, France's natural frontier with Germany. On the west bank stands Strasbourg, France's European city, industrial Mulhouse and picturesque Colmar. Alsace, highly-populated, due to a fairly high birth-rate and people from other areas settling here, is formed from only two departments, Haut-Rhin and Bas-Rhin. About half the population live in the three main cities and a large proportion on the plain beside the Rhine. Here there are innumerable small farm holdings concentrating on vegetables and cereals. Cultivated hills alternate with vineyards, accompanied by delectable little wine towns and villages. Here where the plain meets the foothills of the Vosges is the source of the most prestigious Alsatian wines. Like Lorraine, it has its heavy industry (metallurgical and mechanical), also textiles, chemicals, potash-mining and food-processing, but they are mainly concentrated around its two main cities, Strasbourg and Mulhouse. Thanks to its good geographical position, Alsace has always been well-placed for international trade.

The Vosges, which rise like a buttress between Alsace and Lorraine, measure about 170 kms north to south and are 30 kms at their greatest breadth. The average height is 540 metres: nowhere do they rise higher than 1424 metres. It is a region of dramatic changes. Roads weave through and over the range from whose crests are some magnificent views.

Seen from the Rhine side the Vosges appear as a series of dark hills, a rising wall, especially as you progress further south. The weather is often changeable. Formidable clouds settle along its top, then roll away to reveal blue skies. Seen from Lorraine's open country on the other side, the outline is a wavy line on the horizon, which disappears behind a screen of hills as you approach it. Another oddity is that the northern part is made up of dark, salmon-pink sandstone while the south is of grey granite. The many tiny glacial lakes and trout-filled torrents add their sparkle to the dark foliage — forests of beeches, pines and firs. But in the high Vosges in the south, rounded peaks aptly named 'ballons', which rise dome-like above the trees, are covered with coarse pastureland. The range as a whole is sparsely-populated, the people are concentrated in the valleys, which are usually cultivated. Textile and paper-mills and other small industries which use hydraulic water-power are scattered along the western borders.

The Lorraine side, more directly exposed to the west winds, has a heavier rainfall than the eastern Alsatian side. Snow lies in its valleys longer, spring is later, summer cooler. House styles change as the dark fir forests give way to Lorraine's pretty woodlands and plains. Gabled, flower-decked Alsatian-type houses are replaced by a more traditionally French kind of residence. Even the layout of the towns and villages begins to differ as French influence takes over from Alsatian.

Lorraine is served with a good network of roads, rivers and canals. As in Alsace, farming tends to be on a small-scale due mainly to its harsher climate and more difficult soil. The undulating southern plains have been chiefly taken over by livestock-farming, alternating with woodlands, orchards are lakes, also fields of barley — the favourite cereal crop. There are a few vineyards around Toul and Metz, also at Vic-sur-Seille. Spas, such as Vittel, Contréxeville and Plombières, particularly popular with the French, are to be found in the western foothills of the Vosges.

Northern Lorraine, which we won't be visiting in this book, is highly-populated. The large deposits of coal and iron-ore found here (there are salt deposits around Château Salins and Dieuze) have turned it into an area of heavy industry. Like Britain, until recently, its steel industry was badly hit by the recession. Much of this countryside now appears bleak and forbidding although other types of industries are replacing the older ones. Industry in the south — glassworks, textile and cotton mills — is too dispersed over a wide area to have had much effect on the scenery.

History

Alsace-Lorraine, often spoken of together, is a union of words, due to an accident of history. Neither peoples like to be lumped together. When there you *must* say Alsace AND Lorraine. Both are wealthy and productive, if difficult to defend, and have suffered frequent invasions. Since the 1870s, Alsace and the north-eastern corner of Lorraine have passed backwards and forwards four times between Germany and France. In 1871 to Germany, in 1919 to France, to Germany again in 1940, then back to France in 1945. Yet despite the German-sounding names of some Alsatian places, the south German look of many of the villages, a gutteral accent and the fact that many people now actually commute to work in Germany the two regions are still solidly part of France. The Alsatians, especially, have cultivated the role of being a middle kingdom between two cultures.

Lorraine

Celtic Lorraine, after being conquered by the Romans, then the Franks, became the nucleus of the kingdom of Austrasia. When Charlemagne's empire was divided up in 843, Lothair, who received the middle strip between Rome and the North Sea, gave his name to the kingdom, which became known as Lotharingie (Lotharie Regnum), then Lorraine. However, it lay between powerful neighbours and soon disintegrated into several small states. In 925, Lorraine was added to the Germanic Holy Roman Empire and divided into two duchies, High and Low Lorraine, but eventually the title, 'Lorraine' only applied to High Lorraine. Throughout the Middle Ages, Lorraine along with other Germanic duchies, suffered from the power struggles between the princely families and the great bishoprics (Metz, Toul and Verdun). Although the French kings and the Dukes of Burgundy, both tried to impose their rule over the region, Lorraine managed to remain independent under her own dukes.

French domination of Lorraine dates from the 16th century when control of the duchy became vital in the struggle between France and the Hapsburgs, who ruled the Holy Roman Empire. Lorraine was a battle ground because of its position as a frontier between the two. Union was a slow piecemeal process — individual towns were occupied by French forces. Lorraine was gradually drawn into France's orbit. By the middle of the 18th century, she was definitely attached to France.

The most savage fighting on a scale never seen before in the world's history took place in Lorraine during the First World War. Both sides dug into trenches and lost thousands of men daily to gain or lose a few yards of precious soil. During the Second World War, she had to endure all the horrors of the Nazi regime.

In spite of Lorraine's relatively late entry into France, this province has almost a mystical attachment to the nation. After all, it was the birthplace of Jeanne d'Arc. General de Gaulle (his home was at Colombey-les-Deux-Eglises, near Lorraine's border in Champagne) held the Maid's memory in great reverence. The doubled-barred cross of Lorraine, the emblem of her dukes and a symbol of military courage, was used by the French Resistance movement during the Second World War.

Up to the end of the last century, Lorraine's villages depended chiefly on wood and wheat, orchards and rearing cattle on common pastureland for their livelihoods. The discovery and commercial use of her mineral resources brought about her industrial revolution. Workers from neighbouring countries and provinces emigrated here, considerably increasing her population. By 1912 her output of iron-ore had reached 17 million tons. To gain possession of this vital asset was one reason for the German invasion. The combination of mineral wealth and thermal sources contributed to the region's enduring popularity as a spa centre.

Alsace

The Alsatians are chiefly descended from the Alamans, a Germanic people who, in the 4th and 5th centuries AD, invaded the region. It became part of the loosely-knit kingdom of Lotharingie, then part of the Holy Roman Empire, which split up into smaller units. During that period the territory was divided into a number of ecclesiastical or secular lordships and municipalities, whose boundaries varied over the years, but whose influence persisted until the French Revolution. The period was marked by the growing importance of the cities due to their ever-increasing wealth from trade — which they owed to their geographical position on the Rhine. With the support of the Emperors, who wished to curtail the power of the nobles, the cities were able to emancipate themselves from their feudal overlords. The Burghers of Strasbourg expelled their Bishop Prince after their victory at Oberhausbergen (1262) and many cities in Upper Alsace freed themselves from the control of the Hapsburg princes. Ten Alsatian cities — Haguenau, Landau, Colmar, Sélestat, Wissembourg, Obernai, Rosheim, Kaysersberg, Turckheim, and Munster — formed a union, the Décapole, in 1354 under the protection of the

Holy Roman Emperor who appointed a Landvogt (resident) with his seat at Haguenau. This lasted until Louis XIV's time and did much to give unity to the country and increased their prosperity.

Alsace's most splendid era — except for a bloody peasant revolt in 1525 — was in the 16th century. Her period of greatest misery followed almost immediately in the first part of the 17th century (1618-1648) during the Thirty Years' War when the province was invaded several times and disease and famine were added to the resulting devastation. Alsace turned to France for protection. As a centre of Protestantism, it was administered by 'Intendants' who allowed them a measure of freedom. Louis XIV's Revocation of the Edict of Nantes (which removed many of the former privileges of Protestants) was not applied here, nor were French customs' duties. She was integrated into France properly during the French Revolution and later by Napoleon I. She was confirmed as one of France's frontier regions by the Congress of Vienna in 1815. After the Franco-Prussian war, she was attached to the German empire for 48 years and to Germany again for four years during the Second World War. During this time, the province was treated as German; its young men were drafted into the German army and many were despatched to the Russian front. Dissenters were sent to the German concentration camp at Le Struthof, a very cold place, now preserved as a monument. Some 10,000 people died here during the war.

Alsace could be regarded as a foreign region of France with a culture stemming from German civilization, which has given it its customs, domestic architecture, eating habits and language. Its people are French Germans. Alsatian is a German dialect into which many French words have found their way. Although Alsatians, fiercely individualistic, insist that it is a language on its own, like their architecture. The style of their houses they claim is peculiar to their own province. The Ecology Museum of Upper Alsace, near Mulhouse, shows a variety of Alsatian dwellings ranging from the 13th century to the present day. Most Alsatians speak French, also German. The region is closest culturally to the Black Forest across the Rhine.

The stork is the traditional symbol of Alsace. Many thousands of these tall white birds once bred in parts of Europe, migrating in autumn to return in spring. They were supposed to bring good luck and safety. No house could catch fire with a stork on its roof. People would lay cartwheels across their chimneys so as to give a firm foundation to their nests. Platforms were erected on certain tall buildings. Alas for cosy tradition, only three pairs of storks returned to Alsace in the summer of 1981. This was supposedly due to the draining of marshes (therefore no frogs) and hunting in Africa, their winter home. The Alsatians, anxious to keep their emblem, are trying to rebuild their stork population by mating wild storks with those reared in captivity. If travelling the wine road you will probably pass the one at Kintzheim, near Sélestat. Also, you may be surprised to see, as I was, a single wall occupied by storks at Ostheim (near Riquewihr). Apparently this wall was all that was left of the village after the last war. It remains, standing on its own, as a monument. Somewhat incongruously, storks have chosen this seemingly uncomfortable and eccentric place to nest. Maybe they like being photographed!

Human visitors usually come to Alsace in autumn for the wine festivals and fairs, and in winter to ski down the snow-covered slopes of the Vosges. Old ruined castles on hilltops, open grassy low mountains, woods sloping down to sunny valleys and deep blue lakes, make it a delightful country for long walks, or hiking, in spring, summer and autumn.

Alsatians, more outgoing than their somewhat dour neighbours in Lorraine, are a friendly people. They would like more English visitors. As yet, perhaps because it is inland and less sunny than the south, not many go there. On my last visit, I was usually mistaken for American. It was difficult to find any English newspapers on sale, even at Strasbourg railway station.

Famous People

One of Strasbourg's earliest writers was Godefroy or Gottfried, a lyrical poet. His best known work *The Romance of Tristan and Isolde* (a story he took from Breton legend) was written between 1204 and 1215.

The invention of printing, generally ascribed to Johann Gutenburg (born about 1395 in Mainz) helped to spread the ideas of the Renaissance and the Reformation. Gutenburg came to Strasbourg in 1434 but returned to Mainz in 1444.

His invention was challenged in Strasbourg by Johann Mentelin, who brought out a Bible compressed into fewer pages than Gutenburg's and the first Bible to be printed in German. As the printing industry developed, so did

Strasbourg's reputation as an intellectual centre. The works of Martin Luther were produced here and carried secretly by traders to other parts of France. Strasbourg's democratic character attracted leaders of the Reformation. John Calvin came to live in the city (he was appointed Pastor of the French-speaking church in Strasbourg in 1537), where he met Luther, Melanchthon (German scholar and reformer) and Martin Bucer (celebrated reformer, born in Schlettstadt) and published his articles of faith *L'Institution de la Religion Chrétienne*. An Academy was founded in 1566; the University in 1621. Strasbourg became a front-ranking intellectual and artistic centre.

Nancy was the birthplace of General Hugo (1773-1828), an ardent Napoléonist and father of Victor Hugo; also of Edmund de Goncourt (1822-96), one of the famous Goncourt brothers, who founded the Académe Goncourt, a literary society which annually selects the best imaginative prose work in French for the award of a money prize — *Le Prix Goncourt*.

At Phalsburg was born the writer Emile Erckmann (1822-99). He was the author along with Alexandre Chatrain (1826-90) of novels about Alsatian life. One of the most brilliant journalists of his generation, Edmond About (1828-85) was born at Dieuze. Premier Jules Ferry (1832-93), who promoted free, compulsory, non-clerical education, was born at St-Dié. From Metz came Paul Verlaine (1844-96) one of France's best lyrical poets, and Symbolist poet, Gustave Kahn (1859-1936).

Novelist, essayist and politician, Maurice Barrès (1862-1923), who believed a young Frenchman served his country best in his native province, fostered by his cultural and social roots, was born at Charmes-sur-Moselle. He entered politics as a deputy for Nancy in 1889. His somewhat reactionary views had a considerable influence on France. His works included travel books and a very successful evocative novel, *La Colline Inspirée* (1913), see p. 114-5.

Rather different was the internationalist Robert Schumann (1886-1963) who was both premier and foreign minister. Although born in Luxembourg, he began his political career in 1919, when he was elected deputy for the Moselle department, which he represented in the National Assembly for forty years. His Schumann Plan led to the establishment of the European Common Market. He was President of the European Parliament Assembly from 1958 to 1960. Another practical idealist was Albert Schweitzer (1875-1965), born at Kaysersberg and died in Gabon, theologian, philosopher, organist and mission doctor. Schweitzer was the son of a Lutheran pastor. He studied philosophy and theology at Strasbourg, where he also became an accomplished musician. In 1913 he became a doctor of medicine and set out with his wife, a trained nurse, to Lambaréné in the Gabon province of French equatorial Africa, where he built his first hospital on the Ogooué river. A leper colony was added later. He was awarded the Nobel Peace Prize for his efforts on behalf of the Brotherhood of Nations in 1952.

Martin Schongauer (c1440/50-91), a German painter and engraver, who devoted most of his work to religious subjects, was probably born at Colmar (although Augsberg also claims him). Amongst the few of his paintings which have survived, is his most important 'Madonna in a Rose Garden' (1473) an altarpiece for the church of St Martin in Colmar. Mathias Grunewald (1455-1528), born in West Germany, became court painter to the Archbishop of Mainz, where he received important commissions for altarpieces, such as the 'Issenheim' altarpiece for the Convent of the Antonins of Issenheim (now kept in the Musée d'Unterlinden, Colmar), which is considered his best. Auguste Bartholdi (1834-1904), sculptor of the Lion of Belfort and America's celebrated Statue of Liberty, was born at Colmar (there is a small museum to him there), as was Jean-Jacques Waltz (Hansi) (1873-1951), artist and caricaturist.

The 16th century was a brilliant period for St Mihiel (west of Nancy) which had a famous school attached to its Bénédictine abbey. Sculptor Ligier Richier (1506-67) was born here and he and his descendants — Gerard (1564-1600), Jean, Joseph and Jacob (16th- to 17th-century) — formed the St Mihiel school of sculptors. Other artists produced by the town were Nicholas Cordier (1564-1612) — his works are mainly to be seen in Rome — and Jean Bérain (1640-1711), designer, who headed yet another distinguished artistic family from this area.

Mannerism — a fantastic, luxurious, amusing court style — was especially fashionable in Nancy, capital of Lorraine. Leading figures of this Nancy school were Jacques Callot (1592-1635), Jacques Bellange (c. 1575-1616) and Claude Deruet (1592-1635). Callot was the most celebrated, he was an engraver and draughtsman rather than a painter. After a period working at the Florentine court, he returned to Lorraine in 1621, where he began to turn towards objective realism as is shown by his plates 'Grandes Misères de la Guerre', prompted by the French invasion of the duchy. Jacques Bellange, also more of an engraver than a painter, used its forms to express his passionate religious emotions. Claude Deruet, who was a less interesting artist, left a large number of paintings behind him. These artists' works may be seen in the Musée Historique Lorraine, Nancy.

Some later artists from Nancy were architect Richard Mique (1728-94), Claude Michel (or Clodion) (1738-1814) and portrait-painter J.B. Isabey (1767-1855), who became a court painter. Isabey was a pupil of Jacques Louis David (1748-1825) the famous portraitist and historical painter, active Revolutionist and later court painter to Napoleon.

Claude Lorrain (or Gellée) (1600-82), one of the great 17th-century French painters, was born in a village near Nancy. According to legend, he went to Rome as a pastrycook and took service in the house of landscape painter, Agostino Tassi (1581-1644). He later returned to Lorraine where he was taken on as an assistant to Claude Deruet, then returned to Rome, where he spent the rest of his life, mostly painting the landscape round Rome.

From Lunéville comes artist Jean Girardet (1709-78), while Georges de la Tour (1593-1652) worked for the prosperous bourgeois there for most of his life. Jean Lurcat (1892-1966), artist and designer, was born at Bruyères. The artist-general, Louis François Le Jeune (1775-1848), artist Gustave Doré (1832-83), and sculptor Jean Hans Arp (1886-1965) were born at Strasbourg.

The Epicure's Guide

The narrow plain of Alsace between the mountains of the Black Forest and the Vosges is one of the most fertile regions in all France. Sheltered by the mountains, many crops thrive in the rich soil of the Rhine valley — hops and tobacco, wheat and other cereals, fruit orchards and all kinds of vegetables present a pleasing pattern to the eye. Along the foothills of the Vosges are the vineyards, described by Montaigne in 1580 as 'hillsides covered with most beautifully and carefully tended vines'.

Add the pig and the goose, fish from the Rhine and the mountain streams, cheeses made in the high pastures of the Vosges and you have the essential ingredients of Alsatian cooking. It is basically cold weather peasant food that is diverse in its origins. Some dishes are undoubtedly Germanic, others were brought by the Jews from Poland, Russia and Austria who settled in Strasbourg as early as the 13th century, other influences are clearly French. In Alsace these elements combined effortlessly in a great gastronomic culture, a sturdy, satisfying cuisine of fresh and cured pork, root vegetables and cabbages, breads of all kinds, orchard fruits and mountain berries, but it does not lack sophistication and subtlety. The specialities and traditional dishes of the region are still widely made in homes and restaurants and modern chefs tend to adapt a few ideas of nouvelle cuisine to local dishes rather than import a new style wholeheartedly.

This rather individual cuisine and the way it survives today are typical of a people who have clung to their customs as invaders marched back and forth across their land over the centuries. The sing-song Germanic dialect sprinkled with French words is another example of Alsatian identity, and indeed the people are not French in character — they are calm and reserved, the bustle and chatter of French small towns is absent. The picturesque villages along the Route du Vin with their chalet-like houses and window boxes full of geraniums seem more like Switzerland or Austria.

Choucroute is probably the first dish that comes to mind when Alsatian food is mentioned. It is on restaurant and brasserie menus everywhere and sold in great quantities in charcuteries and in markets to be eaten at home. Choucroute (sauerkraut) is shredded cabbage preserved in salt with seasonings of cloves, bay leaves and juniper, or more rarely these days, cumin, dill and horseradish. Well prepared choucroute is a superb dish; it should be cooked in goose fat and Alsace wine, it should be pale in colour, crunchy and pleasantly acidulated.

After its long slow cooking it is served in a mound surrounded by boiled potatoes and topped with the traditional smoked streaky bacon (lard fumé) and usually another cut of smoked and boiled meat — probably loin chops — and a couple of different sausages. Black pudding sometimes makes an appearance, so does goose confit, a reminder that the Jews of Alsace are choucroute lovers too. A choucroute garnie can be a simple family meal, a basic dish served in a brasserie, or it can be dressed up for grand dinners and the tables of fine restaurants. Autumn is the season of fresh choucroute, when choucroute days are celebrated in Colmar and in the principal producing villages such as Geispolsheim and Krautergersheim.

Choucroute leads naturally to pork, the favourite meat of Alsace. Until early in this century every rural family kept pigs and the village butcher would go from house to house to kill the pig and prepare charcuterie. The annual pig killing was the occasion for a feast to eat the parts that had to be eaten fresh; all the rest was conserved for the winter. Pork appears on the table in many guises: as roast leg or loin or grilled chops; salted or smoked hams, hocks, trotters, belly and shoulder; a vast range of pâtés and sausages, and of course lard is used for cooking.

Charcuterie is the pride of Alsace and the reputation of local producers such that they certainly hold their own against the industrial products on the supermarket shelves. In any village street the window of the charcutier vies with that of the baker as the main attraction. There are fresh sausages for boiling or frying, saucissons secs, blood sausages, bacon, hams, pâtés and terrines, often with dialect, French and German names. Saucisse de Strasbourg, a plump pork and beef version of the frankfurter, is one of the most popular; cervelas, a spiced sausage that once contained pig's brain — hence the name — is another. Tongue, liver and lung are also used to make sausages here. Flavourings vary from place to place but might include onions, raisins, pistachio nuts, truffles and an array of whole spices.

It is said that Alsace has 42 different pâtés and you will find most charcuteries have several all year, but the number increases in the autumn when game is in season. Recipes for pâtés made with game, meat, poultry, fish, snails and fruit are found as early as the 17th century. Today pâté de foie gras is the star, but in the past Alsace was noted for its fish pâtés made with carp, salmon, trout, crayfish or salt cod.

Flocks of geese were kept in both country and town until well into the 20th century. In the park of the Orangerie in Strasbourg is a sculpture of a little goose girl, the Ganseliesel, surrounded by a number of geese eager to eat the vegetables in her basket. These days the geese no longer wander in the charge of the Ganseliesel but are restricted to the farmyard. They are reared primarily for their incomparable foie gras, but they also provide a geat deal of meat and cooking fat, with feathers and quills as by-products. Roast goose, stuffed with apples, or chestnuts, or potatoes and goose liver is served at Christmas and New Year; goose confit, stuffed neck of goose and a stew of neck, wings and gizzards are local specialities.

Fresh foie gras is usually sautéd in butter and garnished with truffles cooked in madeira or apples sautéd in butter. A whole liver studded with truffles may be cooked in a terrine and served cold. It may also be served as a mousse or in aspic, as a garnish for salads or noodles, to stuff goose neck, but its most common form is the pâté de foie gras en croûte. The truffled foie gras is enclosed in a farce of pork and veal and the whole baked in a pastry case. Pâté de foie gras en croûte is said to have been invented by Jean-Pierre Clause, chef to Maréchal de Contades, military governor of Alsace. Clause surrounded the liver with chopped bacon and veal and wrapped the whole in pastry. A great success when first prepared in 1780, it made Clause's fortune: a few years later he married the widow of a patissier and devoted the rest of his life to making and selling his pâté, and a range of others based on venison, hare, wild boar, duck, partridge and quail.

He soon had many imitators in Strasbourg, and one of them, Nicolas-François Doyen, had the idea of using truffles with foie gras, a marriage much appreciated ever since. From these two men developed the whole Alsace foie gras industry. Before leaving the charcuterie, another meat and pastry combination must be mentioned — the tourte, a coarsely chopped mixture of pork and veal, or occasionally ham, baked in a round pie and sold by the slice. Tourte de la Vallée de Munster is one most commonly found, but there are others named after different valleys or towns. They are good country fare.

Cattle have always been raised in the Vosges, but they are raised primarily for their milk. Beef has never been very popular in Alsace, although veal is used. Poultry and game have always been the greatest meats. Chicken and turkey are reared alongside geese, often served with wild mushrooms and cream sauces, although there are also spicy Jewish versions of these dishes without dairy products.

The choice of game is very wide: venison, wild boar, hare, rabbit, pheasant, partridge, wild duck, woodcock and quail are served, perhaps in a civet, a slow-cooked stew, or with the fruits of the region, accompanied by noodles or spaetzle.

Dishes of mixed meats are a feature of Alsace, in particular baeckeoffe, a sustaining winter dish made with pork, pig's trotters, beef and lamb, marinated and then cooked slowly in a casserole with onions, potatoes and sometimes carrots. The name of the dish means baker's oven, for that is where the women took their dish to be cooked in the past while they went to do their weekly wash.

Alsace is still rich in freshwater fish dishes, although the crayfish have long vanished from the streams of the Vosges as well as many fish from the Rhine and the Ill. Fish are farmed and kept in ponds; carp, perch, pike, pike-perch, eel, tench and trout are found on many menus. Look for carpe à la juive, the famous sabbath dish, and matelote à l'alsacienne, an excellent stew of assorted river fish made with the local wine. Some restaurants still prepare the fish pâtés and terrines that were so highly regarded in the past. Frogs' legs have been a delicacy here for centuries; Strasbourg used to have a frog market next to the fish market. Frog soup is a true regional dish. You can also find frogs' legs fried in batter, sautéd with Riesling or served as a delicate mousseline.

Summer is asparagus time in Alsace; the town of Hoerdt has been the asparagus capital of the Bas-Rhin since the end of the 19th century. It is usually served with slices of cooked, raw and smoked ham and three sauces — hollandaise, mayonnaise and vinaigrette. Sorrel, dandelion leaves and nettles gathered in the wild are also likely to appear on summer menus; in autumn come wild mushrooms and in winter root vegetables and cabbage pre-dominate. Horseradish is a favourite condiment; navets confits, turnips pickled in the same way as choucroute, are still found in a few places and onions are used with everything, but particularly well liked in onion tart.

A main course in Alsace is often served with fresh noodles or with spaetzle, small firm curls of dough which are boiled and then fried golden in butter. These are traditional accompaniments to many meat and game dishes and are still made regularly in Alsatian homes. Knepfle, small dumplings made with flour and semolina or with potatoes, rather like gnocchi, used to be the standard Friday main course, served with dried fruit.

Fruits play an important part in the cuisine. All through summer and autumn fruits and berries, both wild and cultivated, are made into tarts, strewn over cakes or pancakes, used to flavour the alcools blancs, or eaux-de-vie, for which the region is renowned. Apples, pears and plums are dried in slices (schnitzen) for winter keeping, to serve with meat and game or to make berawecka, the rich bread of Christmas.

This delicious bread is made from dried pears, quetsch plums, prunes, figs and raisins, flavoured with eau-de-vie and spiced with cinnamon and cloves. It used to be eaten on Christmas Eve before midnight Mass, but now it appears for Christmas breakfast.

The Alsatians are indeed fine patissiers; bredle, a sort of petit four once associated with Christmas, but now available all year round are well worth trying. There are several kinds — anisbredle flavoured with aniseed, butterbredle, a richer version, and schwowebredle and spitzbredle flavoured with almonds. Pretzels, or bretzels as they are called here, both savoury and sweet are served with tea or with a drink in a winstub or wine bar.

Kugelhopf is the universally known cake of Alsace — a light yeast cake with almonds and raisins baked in a special fluted twisted mould. It is served for breakfast, at tea time, as a dessert or to accompany a glass of white wine at any time of the day. The fruit tarts of Alsace outdo other parts of France in the sheer variety of fruits — blueberries, cherries, mirabelles, greengages, quetsch plums, apples, pears and more, often covered with a custard of egg yolk and cream.

The range at the boulangerie is just as immense too. Breads come in all shapes, sizes and flavours — caraway, cumin, aniseed, sweet spices; made with rye, wheat, barley flour; mixed cereal bread, bread with pork fat, bread with nuts, brioche, milk bread and many more.

Thin bread dough is the basis of one of the great homely specialities —

flammekueche, a flat tart spread with cream cheese, cream and eggs and baked in a wood-fired oven. Onions and bacon may be added to a savoury flammekueche or sliced apples to a sweet one. Try it as a snack or as a first course.

Apart from the fresh white cheese, the only notable cheese, common to both Alsace and Lorraine is Munster. The cows spend the summer months in the high pastures of the Vosges and this is where the farm cheeses, which carry an appellation contrôlée, are made.

Summer and autumn are therefore the time when Munster fermier is at its best. The farm cheese is sold unwrapped; the industrial version, which varies little year round, is boxed. Munster is a soft cheese with a red or orange crust and a strong odour. Quite mild when young, the mature cheese is rich and spicy and is usually served with a little dish of caraway seeds. It goes well with the local beer or a glass of muscat.

Strasbourg is certainly the beer capital of France for brewing has flourished in Northern Alsace since the middle ages. Hops and barley are grown on the Rhine plain, and production is about a quarter of the national output. Alsatian beers are of good quality; breweries such as Meteor, Mutzig and Kronenbourg are internationally known and much of their beer is exported. It is also widely appreciated at home and usually drunk from earthenware mugs rather than glasses. In many a brasserie or tavern you will find 20 or 30 very different beers to choose from.

Alsace is the leading producer of fruit liqueurs and eaux-de-vie in France. Every orchard fruit and every wild fruit from the Vosges is distilled. Alcools blancs, or eaux-de-vie are dry, colourless and intensely perfumed with the fruit; liqueurs have an equally perfumed nose, but are sweetish and have a pale colour. The predictable flavours — pear, cherry, apricot, raspberry, quetsch plum, mirabelle are to be found alongside the exotic — sorb, pine bud, elder, holly berry, gentian, rowanberry, mulberry, whitebeam, in every bar, wine shop or supermarket.

The white wines of Alsace are among the best in France. Wines have been made along the foothills of the Vosges for centuries, although halted at intervals by war or revolution. Until the French Revolution the vineyards were largely owned by monasteries and the nobility. When the vineyards were split up, many new owners went for quantity rather than quality and for a hundred years or so Alsatian wines did not fare well. Serious efforts were made to restore quality after 1918 and slowly the vineyards were replanted with the traditional local noble grapes — Riesling, Muscat, Pinot, Gewurztraminer, Tokay, Sylvaner. These efforts have been hugely successful, although recognition in the form of an appellation contrôlée was not granted until 1962.

All Alsace wines are named after the grape variety they are made from. Most of the wines are completely dry, much fuller-bodied than the German wines made from the same grapes, and higher in alcohol. Certain hillside vineyards, distinguished by situation, soil composition and a proven ability to produce outstanding wines have been granted Grand Cru status and this designation appears on the label.

Many Alsace growers also blend their best wines to produce their own quality cuvée, often marked Réserve or Réserve Personnelle. Vendange Tardive wines are made from late harvested grapes which give the wine greater ripeness and richness even though it tastes dry. A tiny amount of dessert wine is produced, these wines are designated Sélection de Grains Nobles.

Riesling is the classic noble grape, producing steely, dry wines of great elegance. It partners fish and poultry dishes well. Tokay-Pinot gris is more full-blown, smoky and nutty and will accompany richly sauced dishes and fresh foie gras. Gewurztraminer is spicy and distinctive, a full-bodied wine to go with full-flavoured food. Muscat, with its perfumed fruit, is hard to pair with food and is usually served as an aperitif, although it can be an admirable foil to a rich, tangy Munster. Pinot blanc and Sylvaner are wines of less pronounced character that make good aperitif and hors d'oeuvre wines.

On the other side of the Vosges in Lorraine life and landscape are rather different. Lorraine is an extension of the Paris basin, a series of côtes or hillsides with large village settlements at their base and pastures above, rising to a wooded plateau, in this case the Vosges. The north of the province is industrial, the south is given over to mixed farming. Vegetables and fruits are plentiful, veal and pork the principal meats, and some excellent charcuterie is produced. Take a look at the stalls in the market at Nancy.

Lorraine is certainly best known for its quiche — the real thing is a savoury custard of eggs and cream and a little bacon in a pastry shell, but today the name has come to mean anything savoury with an egg/cream base that is cooked in pastry. However, a true quiche lorraine is certainly worth searching out for its pure flavours.

Bar-le-Duc is the home of wonderfully clear and fragrant red and white currant jellies, at Commercy the Maison Grojean produces the best madeleines, those little shell shaped cakes that have become famous in literature because the taste of a madeleine dipped in an infusion of tilleul (lime) started Proust on his journey into the past.

The springs of Vittel and Contrexéville are also found in Lorraine, good beer is made and a little wine, but the latter is not drunk outside the region.

Throughout Alsace and Lorraine there are special foods for religious and secular festivals. Breads and cakes are particularly associated with the great religious holidays; but the patron saints of the villages, of the vineyards (St Urbain) of hunters (St Hubert) are all celebrated on their day. On the secular side Ribeauvillé has a kougelhopf festival, Munster a tourte festival, Mirecourt one for the quiche, Osenbach one for the snail, Vittel, a frog fair and there are many more to celebrate hops, cherries, plums, cheesecake — all occasions for good eating and drinking.

Handy Tips

HOW TO GET THERE FROM THE UK

The Itinerary begins at Strasbourg. The swiftest way, although expensive, is to fly or rail to Strasbourg, hire a car (booked in advance) which can be left at Metz on your departure. Fly or rail back to UK. Alternatively by car from the UK, Dover-Calais, then take the autoroutes A26/A4 direct to Strasbourg. However, all channel crossings tend to become heavily booked, therefore we heartily recommend making an early reservation.

WHEN TO GO

Any time from Easter to the end of September. In a good Autumn, warm sunny weather will last to the end of October.

Try to avoid travelling on or just before or after a bank holiday (see below). The worst time for traffic is the first weekend in August, when nearly every French family is on the move.

HOTELS

It is advisable to book hotels in advance especially between July and September, particularly when your visit coincides with the wine festivals.

CAMPING AND CARAVANNING

There are some wonderful sites throughout France. Buy the green Michelin Camping and Caravanning guide for addresses. Unlike dreary England even the smallest of sites has electricity. N.B. Don't forget your Caravan Club of Great Britain registration carnet.

DRIVING

Driving on the right is usually no problem, the danger only comes when returning to the road from a car park, a petrol station and of course at roundabouts. Until recently priority was always given to those approaching from the right. This custom is fast changing and roundabouts can therefore be treated in the English style, but beware drivers turning from small roads in towns and country lanes. Traffic police can be tough even on foreign motorists who are caught speeding, overshooting a red light or failing to wear seat belts, so take care. Seat belts are obligatory everywhere in France outside town limits.

ROAD NUMBERS

The French government, which used to be responsible for numbering all the roads in France, has started to hand over the responsibility to the individual départements. In their wisdom the individual départements have in some cases decided to renumber the roads and as you can imagine this process is not only slow but confusing. I have tried to be as correct as possible with the road numbers, but you may unfortunately find some discrepancies. For example you could come across a road marked as the N137 when it is really the D937.

SPEED LIMITS

Autoroutes	130 kmph (80 mph)
Other Roads	90 kmph (56 mph)
Dual Carriageways	110 kmph (68 mph)
Built-up areas or as directed by signs	60 kmph (37 mph)

Autoroutes nearly all have periodic tolls (péages) and can be expensive on long journeys.

THE METRIC SYSTEM

Kilometres — for road distances 8 km equals 5 miles thus:

Km:miles	Km:miles	Km:miles	Km:miles
3:2	8:5	40:25	90:56
4:2½	9:5½	50:31	100:62
5:3	10:6	60:37	125:78
6:3½	20:12	70:44	150:94
7:4	30:18	80:50	200:125

BANK HOLIDAYS

New Years' Day	1st January
Easter Monday	Variable
Labour Day	1st May
V.E. Day	8th May
Ascension Day	6th Thursday after Easter
Whit Monday	2nd Monday after Ascension

Bastille Day	14th July
Assumption	15th August
All Saints (Toussaint)	1st November
Armistice Day	11th November
Christmas Day	25th December

BANKS

Banks are shut on Saturdays and Sundays, except in towns with a Saturday market, when they open on Saturday and shut on Monday. Banks also close at midday on the eve of bank holidays. Banking hours are normally 8 a.m.-12 noon and 2-4.30 p.m. When changing cheques or travellers' cheques remember your passport and Eurocheque encashment card or other internationally recognised cheque card.

SHOP OPENING TIMES

These vary according to a) season b) type of shop c) size of town. In most places shops are open on Saturday, but may be shut on Monday. Food shops (baker, butcher, general store) tend to shut later than others, sometimes as late as 7 p.m., some open on Sundays and bank holiday mornings. Generally all shops close for 2-3 hours at lunchtime from midday.

TRANSPORT

S.N.C.F. — Société Nationale de Chemin de Fer. The trains are generally very clean, comfortable and punctual. It is best to buy tickets in advance from mainline stations or travel agents. Seats can be reserved on main lines. Hire cars can be booked in advance in most large towns. Bicycles can be hired at stations. Men over 65 and women over 60 should purchase a Rail Europ S (RES), from British Rail. This will entitle you to a 50% reduction on fares. Hoverspeed (UK) and Sealink (UK) also provide reduced fares.

Note: Many stations have automatic red punch ticket machines on the platform, this dates your ticket. If you do not get your ticket punched by one of these machines you can be charged again, plus a fine of 20%, so be careful.

MONUMENTS AND MUSEUMS

Opening times and prices of admission have not been included in this book, as they are subject to change. All places mentioned are open to the public and will charge a few francs admission. Normally they will be open from Easter to the end of October, from 9.30-12.00 a.m. and from 3-5 p.m.

Note: Guided tours will cease admission half an hour before closing. Check with the local tourist office for details.

KEY TO ITINERARY
Ratings are for prices/room/night.

★★	Reasonable	★★★★	Expensive
★★★	Average	★★★★★	Very expensive

Names of the hotels and restaurants are printed in bold and are distinguished by the following symbols:

Lunch   Dinner

The itinerary provides a basic route for each day and, for those with time available, offers suggestions for additional trips marked in the text as *Detours*.

Maps
The map on p. 10 shows the complete itinerary.
The daily routes are mapped in detail as follows:
Days 1-5:   p. 46
Days 6-9:   pp. 82-3
Days 10-13: pp. 108-9

At the beginning of each day in the Itinerary there is a summary of the route to be taken, and grid references of the places visited. Grid references are given longitude first, then latitude (i.e. reading from the perimeter of the map, the horizontal numbers, then the vertical). Each square represents 10′.

We recommend you use Michelin Series 1/200,000-1cm:2km, nos. 241 and 242 to accompany your travels.

Metz Cathedral

The Itinerary

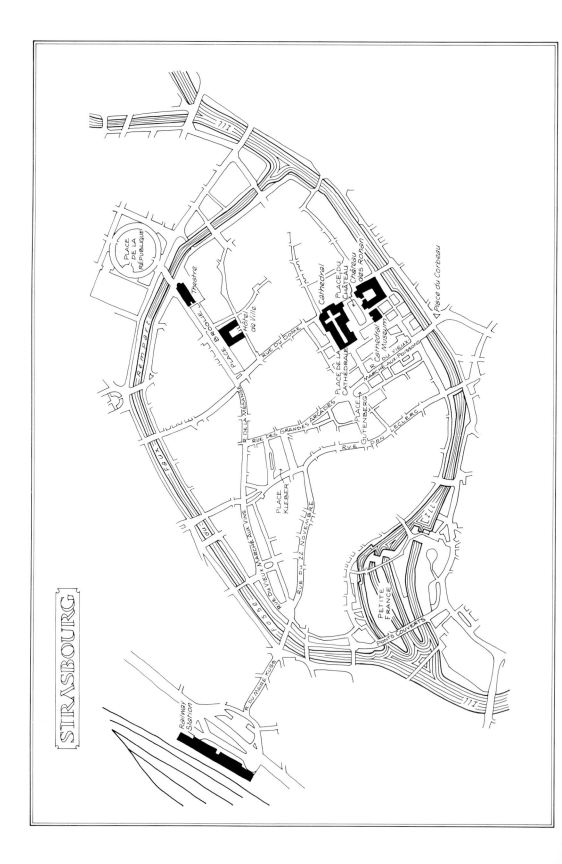

STRASBOURG

Railway Station

R. DU MAIRE KUSS

F O S S É

RUE DU VIEUX MARCHÉ AUX VINS

OU

RUE DU 22 NOVEMBRE

PLACE KLÉBER

RUE DE LA MÉSANGE

RUE DES GRANDES ARCADES

RUE DU DÔME

PLACE BROGLIE

Théâtre

Hôtel de Ville

Fb UXG

Rempart

PLACE DE LA RÉPUBLIQUE

Cathedral

PLACE DU CHÂTEAU

Château des Rohan

Place du Corbeau

PLACE DE LA CATHÉDRALE

Cathedral Museum

R. DU VIEUX

MARCHÉ-AUX-POISSONS

PLACE GUTENBERG

RUE DU PON LECLERC

PETITE FRANCE

PONTS COUVERTS

I L L

DAY 1

The itinerary begins with a day spent in Strasbourg — a lively, cosmopolitan city. Perhaps more importantly, as regards the tour which follows, Strasbourg is the capital and centre of Alsace and so serves as an excellent introduction to a holiday in the region.

Overnight in Strasbourg.

Map reference
Strasbourg   7°45'E 48°35'N

Maison Kammerzell, Strasbourg

Arrive Strasbourg

Strasbourg

The banks on the Rhine's French side are lower than those on the German one and are more liable to flooding. Thus Alsatian cities, such as Mulhouse, Colmar, Sélestat, even Strasbourg — although its suburbs lie beside it — have been built some miles to the west. The river usually shown in pictures of Strasbourg is the Ill, a stream which runs parallel to the Rhine until it joins it above Strasbourg. The Ill is the river from which the name Alsace originated 'Ill Sass'.

Strasbourg, honeycombed by the Ill's tributaries, is connected by numerous bridges. A city of many rôles, it is an ancient university town, a port, a celebrated art centre and both Europe's and Alsace's capital city. It is also the headquarters of the European Court of Justice and the European Science Foundation.

As Parliamentary and conference delegates, officials connected with EEC business and tourists compete for accommodation, one should not arrive here without having booked one's hotel first. Euro-MPs sit five days a month: there are no sessions in August; two in October.

Strasbourg had humble beginnings. About 800 BC it was a fishing village on an island surrounded by the Ill. The Romans turned the village into a camp which commanded the crossing of the Rhine at the junction of roads leading into Gaul, Germania and Italia. The rectangular shape of their castrum can still be seen in the pattern of some of today's streets and drains. The forum and temple were situated where the city's cathedral now stands. The Roman town took the Celtic name Argentoratum (the river Ill was originally called Argens), but its present name, Strasbourg — city of crossroads — comes from the Merovingian period.

The great days of Strasbourg started in the early 13th century, when under the rule of its Bishops it became a powerful city. It was proud of its riches, its liberty and most especially its cathedral, whose delicate 142 metres spire dominates the city and Alsatian plain. It was added in 1439, one hundred years after the main building, and was hailed as a wonder of the world, the loftiest spire in Christendom. The platform has a good view over the Rhine.

Today's crowds of sightseers, usually armed with clicking cameras, and gathered in the cobble-stoned Place de la Cathédrale unfortunately rather diminish the medieval atmosphere so well engendered by the surrounding old gabled houses. At night, strolling couples, arms entwined, and performers — musicians and mummers — set against the backdrop of arched passageways and delightfully lop-sided houses, walls glowing pink from behind wooden beams, perhaps bring it more successfully to life. Cathedral bells toll occasionally, their timeless tirade to remind us that we are all mortal and will eventually pass away.

The cathedral is built out of local pinkish grey sandstone. In spite of fires and bombardments, its splendid Gothic facade has managed to survive much as it was conceived by Erwin de Steinbach. The richly-carved intricate central portal, showing scenes from the Bible, is surmounted by a superb rose window. The portal on the right contains statues of the wise and foolish virgins: that on the left, vices and virtues. A door on the right facade leads to the famous astronomical clock (Schwilge, 1838) with its noonday parade of allegorical figures.

To note especially inside are the 13th-century Doomsday pillar, depicting angels weeping on the Day of Judgement, carved by an unknown sculptor from Chartres; the magnificent 17th-century tapestries representing scenes from the life of the Virgin; and 12th- to 14th-century stained glass windows.

Visitors to Strasbourg are fortunate in that its main places of interest — the cathedral and museums — are not very far apart. Outside the cathedral, facing its north front, is the Pharmacie du Cerf, the oldest chemist shop in France (dates from 1268); while on the northwest side of the square is Maison Kammerzell (1467-1589), now a very good restaurant, and whose front is the best example of a carved facade in the town. On the other side of the cathedral in the Place du Château, is the cathedral museum, housed in two wings of the former Maison de l'Oeuvre and the old Hôtellerie du Cerf, clustered round four little courtyards. The museum is devoted to Alsatian art of the medieval and Renaissance period. The Château des Rohan, nearby, was built in 1742 and named after 4 members of the Rohan family who were Bishops here. Now the Château houses museums. The Museum of Decorative Arts occupies the Grand Apartments on the ground floor and includes 18th-century furniture and ceramics, many from Strasbourg and Nidewiller. On the floor above, the Museum of Fine Arts displays an important collection of pictures.

If you continue down to the quayside, you will come to where the boat trips start, a good introduction to the city. A pleasant way to spend an evening is to take a trip, plus a meal, on the boat.

A favourite place to visit when in Strasbourg is Petite France (also known as Bain-aux-Plantes), a curious old quarter, once chiefly occupied by tanners, stituated amid the city's canals and waterways, near Ponts Couverts (its four square towers are part of the remains of the city's ramparts). To get the full flavour of this old quarter, whose towers, turrets and gables are mirrored so peacefully in the water, you need to wander round slowly, especially in the evening.

The old Alsatian houses with carved wooden facades, inner courtyards and turrets, have mostly been restored to picturesque medieval quaintness. Note the holes in the roofs of many of the houses in which pigeons were kept. Pigeons were used to carry post, especially during times of trouble.

Strasbourg has many fine squares. In the Place Gutenburg is a statue to the pioneer printer. In Place Kléber, its largest and most celebrated one, stands a statue to General Kléber (born in Strasbourg 1753, assassinated in Cairo 1800). In Place de la République is a monument to those who died in the 1914-18 war, and in Place Broglie, a monument to General Le Clerc, who liberated Strasbourg in 1944.

In Place Broglie also look out for the plaque on the wall of the Banque de France in memory of the man whose famous song inspired France with patriotism. After the Revolution, when France had declared war on Prussia and Austria, the French army was stationed at the ready in Strasbourg. During an Officers' banquet the Mayor suggested to a young officer, Rouget de l'Isle, known to be a poet and musician, that he write a good marching song for the army. The young man agreed, sat up all night, then handed the Mayor the song *Chant de Guerre de l'Armée du Rhin*. The Mayor liked it, numerous copies were printed, and it was later sung by volunteers marching to Paris from Marseilles. The *Marseillaise* as it was eventually known became France's national anthem.

The Parliament of Europe, housed in a new somewhat strange-looking, glassy angular building, was founded in 1949 in the hope that it would help to unite Europe. One of its first projects was the Schumann Plan, which pooled Europe's coal and steel resources in 1951. It is the headquarters of the

Council of Europe (an organisation of 20 member states, quite separate from the Common Market) as well as being the main venue of the European Parliament and so one of the EEC's three capitals, along with Brussels and Luxembourg.

There are city tours on offer by day or evening, and you can join organised tours easily. The Tourist Office will be happy to give details of what is available during your visit. Trips may be made to the port on the Rhine and down the Rhine. There are daily tours into the region, or into neighbouring Germany. For these, visit the blue office (left side, coming out of the station). The best place to pick up local buses is Place Kléber. Buses go from here to the airport, about 15 kms away. The No. 9 will take you to Strasbourg main station.

Dinner and overnight in Strasbourg.

Maison Kammerzell
16 Place Cathédrale
67000 Strasbourg
Tel: (88) 32 42 14

One of the listed sights of the town, a spectacular 5-storey, timber-framed building in most exuberant Alsatian style. Well worth a visit for a drink and a look around but there are more economical places to eat.

Instead try Restaurant Zum Strissel, close by the Cathedral Square. In its way an equally amazing timber-framed building. You can hardly believe how it all stands up. This offers genuine Alsace cuisine with a choice of menus. The wine list is mainly Alsatian and happily serves several by the quarter-litre carafe. Very good value.

Restaurant Zum Strissel
5 Place de la Grande Boucherie
67000 Strasbourg
Tel: (88) 32 14 73

Closed:	Sunday and Monday
Credit cards:	Carte Bleu, Visa, Am.Ex.
Food:	Try their onion tart, an inexpensive but delicious treat.
Rating:	★★

Hotel de l'Europe
38 Rue du Fosse des Tanneurs
67000 Strasbourg
Tel: (88) 32 17 88

Old, yet comfortable, it is situated in the heart of the town. You would be in good company as philosopher and writer Voltaire and German poets, Goethe and Schiller, are supposed to have once stayed here. Traffic is not particularly noisy at night although you might hear the celebratory songs of revellers wending their way home. But you cannot expect everything!

Its owner, a third generation one, Patrick Diebold, speaks excellent English.

Closed:	Open all year
Rooms:	60
Facilities:	Bar (no restaurant), television in rooms
Credit cards:	Am.Ex, Diners, Mastercard, Access, Visa, Carte Bleu
Rating:	★★★

Hôtel Cathédrale
12 Place de la Cathédrale
67000 Strasbourg
Tel: (88) 22 12 12

Closed:	Open all year
Rooms:	32
Facilities:	Television, telephones in all rooms
Credit cards:	Am.Ex, Euro, Diners
Rating:	★★★

STRASBOURG: USEFUL INFORMATION

Tourist Office:	Palais des Congrès Avenue Shutzenberger Tel: (88) 35 03 00
and	Place Gare Tel: (88) 32 51 49
and	Place Gutenberg Tel: (88) 32 57 07
Population:	252,264
Facilities:	Golf Course (4km), Airport (12km)
Interest:	Cathedral, ancient buildings, museums, châteaux, port tours by boat

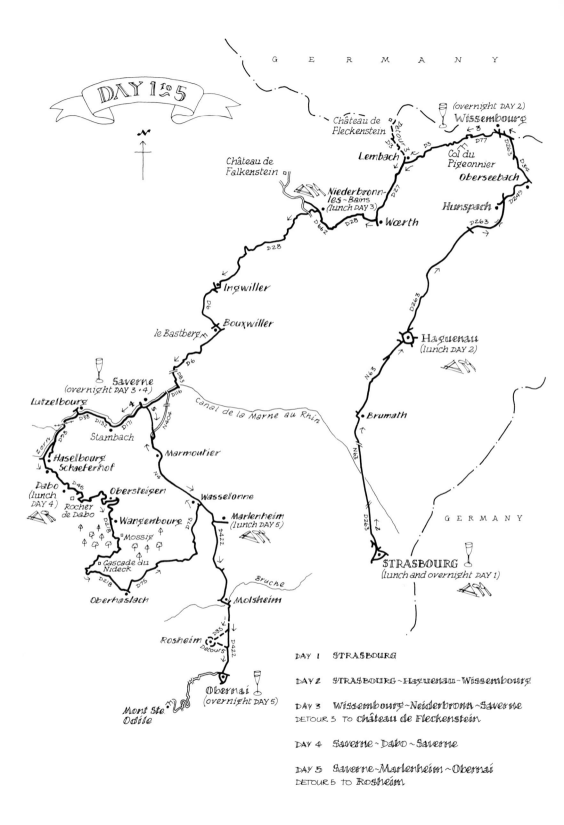

GERMANY

DAY 1 to 5

N

GERMANY

Château de Fleckenstein
(overnight DAY 2)
Wissembourg
Lembach
Col du Pigeonnier
Oberseebach

Château de Falkenstein
Niederbronn-les-Bains
(lunch DAY 3)
Wœrth
Hunspach

Ingwiller
Bouxwiller
le Bastberg

Saverne
(overnight DAY 3 + 4)
Lutzelbourg
Stambach
Hasellbourg
Schaeferhof
Marmoutier

Haguenau
(lunch DAY 2)

Brumath

Canal de la Marne au Rhin

Dabo
(lunch DAY 4)
Rocher de Dabo
Obersteigen
Wangenbourg
Mossig
Cascade du Nideck
Oberhaslach

Wasselonne
Marlenheim
(lunch DAY 5)

GERMANY

STRASBOURG
(lunch and overnight DAY 1)

Bruche
Molsheim

Rosheim
Détours

Obernai
(overnight DAY 5)
Mont Ste Odile

DAY 1   STRASBOURG

DAY 2   STRASBOURG ~ Haguenau ~ Wissembourg

DAY 3   Wissembourg ~ Neiderbronn ~ Saverne
DÉTOUR 3 TO Château de Fleckenstein

DAY 4   Saverne ~ Dabo ~ Saverne

DAY 5   Saverne ~ Marlenheim ~ Obernai
DÉTOUR 5 TO Rosheim

DAY 2

Strasbourg, Haguenau, Wissembourg: approx. 62 km (39 miles)

Leaving Strasbourg the route heads towards the gentle northern Vosges by the German frontier. Stopping at Haguenau for lunch, then meandering through some traditional flower-decked Alsace villages, the day ends at Wissembourg, renowned for its 16th-century old quarter ringed by the Lauter river.

Overnight at Wissembourg.

Map references
Strasbourg	7°45′E 48°35′N
Haguenau	7°48′E 48°49′N
Hunspach	7°57′E 48°57′N
Oberseebach	7°59′E 48°58′N
Wissembourg	7°57′E 49°02′N

Breakfast at Strasbourg.

Vosges du Nord

The hills of the northern Vosges, the 'Little Vosges', which rarely rise much above 1000 feet, lie beyond the Bruche valley. This is the domain of red sandstone, so very useful in the construction of the châteaux, churches and cathedrals of the region. Erosion has bitten into many of its rocky heights causing curious shapes, yet contributing to the picturesque craggy country-side, with its castles, little towns and villages, and roads winding through fir forests.

The Parc Naturel Régional des Vosges du Nord stretches along the frontier with Germany. Hills dotted with ruined castles, such as Falkenstein and Fleckenstein, reflect the region's violent past.

From Strasbourg, take the D263 and N63 to Haguenau, a busy commercial town beside the Moder river. It was one of the ten cities of the Décapole and used to be surrounded by forests, which were believed to be holy. The Druids consecrated it to their Gods and in later Christian times it became the home of hermits the effects of whose simple lives and preaching continued long after the barbarian armies had swept by. Today's forest only lies to the north of the town. From the road you will probably see hopfields, along with those of maize, tobacco, wheat and sunflowers, for Haguenau is noted for its beer.

Haguenau

It was a favourite residence of the Emperor Frederick Barberouse. Today the town has a pleasant holiday atmosphere in spite of the commerce. It has quite an interesting Alsatian museum (collection of furniture, pottery and household objects) situated in a restored 15th-century building in the pedestrianised area, and two churches, St Nicholas (founded by the emperor in 1189 and added to and restored in the 13th, 14th and 18th (wood carvings) centuries) and St George (12th- and 13th-century, bombarded 1945, restored 1963) which has a sturdy air. To note especially is its retable of the Last Judgement, 1496. I shall always remember St George because it was here that I slipped and hurt my ankle. Later, at Wissembourg, I bought a most fascinating walking stick, which unscrewed into three parts. The handle was quite intriguing. When removed it revealed a small but very sharp knife. Was this intended to be used for 'manger' or 'La défense'?

Lunch at Haguenau.

Follow the D263 to Hunspach, very clean, colourful and orderly. The villages around here are known as the Villages Fleuris because of their flower-decked houses and decorations — SNCF buses do a tour around them about once a week. They each have their own particular charm and are as interesting in their own way as the wine ones further south.

Take the D249 to Oberseebach, another typical Alsatian village. You may be lucky and see people wearing their national dress — the practice is most common on Sundays for morning church. Then the D34 and D263 to Wissembourg.

Wissembourg

This is a truly delightful town: its old houses are a good example of 16th-century Alsatian architecture. It first evolved around its Bénédictine abbey. Armed with a map from the tourist office in the Town Hall I recommend you just stroll around enjoying the atmosphere. The old town is surrounded by the River Lauter which is crossed by innumerable little bridges as it weaves between the houses.

Start at the Town Hall, built 1741-52, to replace the old Rathaus, burned down in 1677: then pass the Maison du Sel, near a bridge, once a hospital, then a salt depot, an abbatoir and a hospital for sick soldiers. After crossing the bridge, continue along the quayside, turning right past Lycée Stanislas and Hôpital Stanislas.

Stanislas the Magnificent came here with his daughter Marie after losing his Polish throne. He was sad, poor and badly in debt. Imagine his delight when in 1725, after spending six years in Wissembourg, the Duke of Antin arrived from Paris with the remarkable news that Louis XV had chosen his Marie to be Queen of France. It was not really the King's choice; she was selected by the Duke of Bourbon and his mistress, who believed she might be easy to use. Their marriage took place by proxy in Strasbourg cathedral — the 15-year-old Louis was in Paris. Marie was 22. She bore him three daughters.

Complete the circle, passing the Sous Préfecture, built 1784, and you will come to dignified St Pierre and St Paul, reckoned to be the grandest Gothic church in Alsace after Strasbourg cathedral. Built 1262-93 it was the abbey church of Wissembourg. Its interior is remarkable for the purity of its classical Gothic proportions. For interest, note the fresco, 12 metres high, of St Christopher, which was discovered fairly recently and restored.

Beside the river there are innumerable walks. The Bruche quarter is particularly attractive, also the garden on the Promenade des Remparts. If interested in history and archaeology, you might care to visit the Musée Westercamp.

Wissembourg is on the border with Germany and is very popular with the Germans, possibly because the dialect spoken here is almost the same as their own.

Dinner and overnight at Wissembourg.

HAGUENAU: USEFUL INFORMATION

Tourist Office:	1 Place J-Thierry
	Tel: (88) 73 30 41
Population:	29,715

WISSEMBOURG: USEFUL INFORMATION

Tourist Office:	Hôtel de Ville
	Tel: (88) 94 10 11
Population:	6,536
Interest:	Traditional architecture and church

Hôtel Barberousse
8 Place Barberousse
67500 Haguenau
Tel: (88) 73 31 09

Two fixed price menus change daily and represent the best selection of the chef's cuisine.

Closed:	Sundays and Mondays
Credit cards:	Euro, Visa
Food:	Genuine Alsatian with several international dishes.
Rating:	★★★

Hôtel L'Ange
2 Rue de la République
67160 Wissembourg
Tel: (88) 94 12 11

A small hotel with a pretty garden by the river.

Closed:	Sunday evenings and Mondays
Rooms:	8
Facilities:	Garden, telephones in rooms
Food:	Very good value
Rating:	★★

Hôtel La Walck
2 Rue de la Walck
67160 Wissembourg
Tel: (88) 94 06 44

A slightly larger hotel but which also has a shaded garden and riverside views, and a terrace overlooking the lake.

Closed:	15-30 January, 15-30 June, Sunday evenings and Mondays
Rooms:	15
Facilities:	Garage parking, telephones
Food:	Regional specialities
Rating:	★★★

Niederbronn-les-Bains

DAY 3

Wissembourg, Niederbronn-les-Bains, Saverne: approx 70 km (44 miles)

From Wissembourg, drive to Lembach where you can visit some bunkers from the Maginot Line installations, or perhaps detour a little to the north to see a more ancient stronghold — the ruins of castle Fleckenstein. After stopping at Niederbronn-les-Bains for lunch head south to Saverne.

Overnight at Saverne.

Map references

Wissembourg	7°57′E 49°02′N
Lembach	7°47′E 49°00′N
Castle Fleckenstein	7°46′E 49°02′N
Woerth	7°45′E 48°57′N
Niederbronn-les-Bains	7°39′E 48°58′N
Ingwiller	7°29′E 48°53′N
Bouxwiller	7°29′E 48°49′N
Saverne	7°22′E 48°45′N

Route shown p. 46.

Breakfast at Wissembourg.

Wissembourg was a centre of the last war's Maginot Line (comprised of tunnels, underground forts, strong walls and gun emplacements), France's white elephant. The Germans simply encircled it and took over its defences. Parts of the Line's installations may be visited, there are bunkers at nearby Lembach open to the public.

Drive first towards Lembach, D3, (one of Alsace's prettiest villages) passing Col du Pigeonnier from whose belvédère are extensive views over the Alsatian plain and Black Forest.

All along the west German border is attractive. Steep wooded hills and rocky heights, often crowned by crumbling castles, rise along the Regional Park. It is an empty country, a sort of no-man's land. The nearby castles of Falkenstein (used as a 19th-century prison for Frenchmen) and Fleckenstein (has a small museum) are magnificent viewpoints. These medieval strongholds of powerful rulers remain as obsolete symbols of yesterday's defences, of interest not only to historians, but also to artists and lovers of the quaint and picturesque. Legends and folklore abound.

Detour

At Lembach after visiting the last war's defences you could follow the D3 northwards and turn right to visit the ruins of 13th-century Fleckenstein. Return to Lembach.

Woerth

Take the D27 to Woerth, once the residence of the Counts of Hanau. The important battle of Woerth-Froeschwiller (Franco-Prussian war, 1870/1) was fought near here. You can visit the museum dedicated to this event — uniforms, arms, equipment, documents, etc. — in the Town Hall and make a tour of the battlefields where German and French monuments have been built to commemorate those who died.

Niederbronn-les-Bains

Next take D28 and D662 to Niederbronn-les-Bains. All around here is splendid mountain scenery. The town evolved around its two springs, used both by Celts and Romans and is now a large spa. It became prosperous during the time of the Second Empire (1851-1870) but was unfortunately badly damaged during the last war. It is now restored and attracts those suffering from rheumatism and arthritis (the Roman spring in the heart of the town) and gout and obesity (Celtic spring, north of the railway station). Niederbronn-les-Bains encourages active and sporting holidays. It is equipped with large green parks, tennis courts, a swimming pool and signposted hikes through the surrounding woods. For those less healthily inclined there is a casino. Niederbronn makes a good base for those wishing to explore this region. Nearby are the ruins of Windstein, Falkenstein, Wintersberg and Wasenbourg castles.

Lunch at Niederbronn-les-Bains.

Continue on the D28 to Ingwiller (note its synagogue surmounted by an odd-looking greenish-grey dome), then the D6 to Bouxwiller, a little town at the foot of the Bastberg. Its fortifications were dismantled in the 17th century and its château destroyed during the Revolution. To note here are old houses (16th- to 17th-century) and the 17th-century Alsatian Renaissance Town Hall.

Saverne

Follow the D6 to Saverne on the Zorn, a small town most strategically placed at the foot of ruined Haut Barr (well-called the 'eye of Alsace') and Haut Griffin, two fortresses, and a natural gateway through the mountains in the west to Alsace.

Saverne is another delightful and colourful Alsatian town and a good place to spend a couple of nights. Park your car in front of the Château des Rohan, a severely French style building in pinkish-brown stone. There are two gate-houses in front: one houses the Information Office. Go inside and collect the pink map and information sheet (in English) and other pamphlets telling you what to do and see in and around the town.

If the Château is closed (between 12 and 2) you can visit the parochial church above. From the 13th century to the Revolution, Saverne belonged to the Prince Bishops of Strasbourg. Cardinal Prince Louis-René de Rohan was responsible for this château, built after a fire in the 18th century, and he lived here in grand style. At the back pillars, high windows and a balustraded terrace overlook a formally laid-out garden.

Saverne the town took over the château in 1814 and later sold it to the state. It became an apartment house for widows of officers, then a barracks. It is now an ancient monument. There is a museum on the second floor, showing paintings and sculptuary, pictures of the old town, archaeological remains, also portraits of royalty, of Cardinal Armand Gaston du Rohan Soubise (1708-49) and one of Marie Leczinska (Stanislas's daughter), who may well have stayed here with her husband, Louis XV. The rooms are spacious but not ornate.

Saverne is surrounded by water and crossed by little bridges. Follow Grande Rue with its old houses, and usually some balconies ablaze with flowers adding their brightness to the flags strung across the street. I suggest a visit to the Rosarie, off the Route de Paris. Here you will find 1200 varieties of roses, old and new, all sizes and scents, a glorious array of pinks, reds, yellows and whites. Wedding photos are sometimes taken here. Cold drinks are sold at the entrance: there are plenty of scattered seats around for a picnic.

It was at Saverne, incidentally, that the Revolt of the Rustauds (peasants) was put down in the 16th century. They were trying to shake off their feudal ties. After being besieged here by the Duke of Lorraine, they eventually gave in on the understanding that their lives be spared. Alas, they were cut down and brutally murdered by the Duke's men.

Dinner and overnight at Saverne.

NIEDERBRONN-LES-BAINS:
USEFUL INFORMATION

Tourist Office:	Place Hôtel de la Ville
	Tel: (88) 09 17 00
Population:	4,476
Facilities:	Casino, spa

Restaurant Les Acacias
35 Rue des Acacias
67110 Niederbronn-les-Bains
Tel: (88) 09 00 47

There are many restaurants to choose from in this spa town, but for charm, good value and fine food Les Acacias must be a favourite. A gingerbread house surrounded by trees and flowers, the chef and proprietor Noel Dontenville offers elegant food at very reasonable prices.

Closed:	21-31 December, February, Monday evenings and Tuesdays
Credit cards:	Am.Ex, Visa, Carte Bleu
Food:	Try Papillotte de Sandre au Foie Gras, or Champignons Gratinés à l'Escargot
Rating:	★★

SAVERNE: USEFUL INFORMATION

Tourist Office:	Château des Rohan Tel: (88) 91 80 47
Population:	10,484
Interest:	Château, old buildings, rosarium

Hôtel Restaurant 'Boeuf Noir'
22 Grand Rue
67700 Saverne
Tel: (88) 91 10 53

A friendly-looking hotel right in the centre of town. The food is interesting and extremely good value, specialising in regional dishes.

Closed:	Sunday evenings and Tuesdays
Rooms:	18
Facilities:	Telephones, parking
Credit cards:	Euro, Visa, Carte Bleu
Food:	Try Choucroute aux Poissons, Panache de Poisson and Cordon de Veau à la Strasbourgeoise
Rating:	★★

Hôtel Restaurant Geiswiller
17 Rue de la Côte
67700 Saverne
Tel: (88) 91 18 51

Another pleasant, white painted establishment. This hotel has the added attraction of a tree-shaded terrace for diners on warm summer evenings.

Closed:	Open all year
Rooms:	41
Facilities:	Private parking, televisions and telephones in rooms
Credit cards:	Am.Ex, Diners, Visa
Food:	Seasonal specialities include Foie Gras Chaud aux Renettes from October to March, and fresh game from June to January.
Rating:	★★★

DAY 4

Saverne, Wangenbourg, Saverne: 82 km (51 miles)

A round trip from Saverne offers the opportunity to enjoy the attractive scenery this part of the Vosges offers — a mixture of forests, fertile valleys and rivers overlooked by castle ruins from the hilltops.

Overnight at Saverne.

Map references

Saverne	7°22′E 48°45′N
Stambach	7°18′E 48°44′N
Haselbourg	7°13′E 48°42′N
Dabo	7°14′E 48°39′N
Wangenbourg	7°18′E 48°37′N
Nideck	7°16′E 48°35′N
Oberhaslach	7°20′E 48°33′N
Marmoutier	7°24′E 48°42′N

Route shown p. 46.

Breakfast at Saverne.

The Dabo-Wangenbourg region is one of the prettiest parts of the Vosges. It is a wild yet gentle countryside: leafy and rocky heights, both grey and pink, alternate with fresh valleys, rivers and rushing streams, protected — or more likely dominated — by ruined hilltop feudal castles.

From Saverne, drive along the D132, following the wooded Zorn valley, a route well-known since early times for crossing through to Lorraine. You will pass Stambach, then the remains of Lutzelbourg castle, and a few kilometres further on, the canal Louis-Arzviller. Before (D98, D45) Schaeferhof (a village popular with trout-fishers), the village of Haselbourg, perched on a hill, appears. Further along the D45 and overlooking the picturesque valley of Grossthal, looms the rock of Dabo itself.

Dabo

From this grey-red pedestal (664 metres) are sweeping views over the countryside. One can see the Vosges principal grey summits, such as the Schneeberg (favourite meeting place for Vosgien witches), Grossmann and the imposing dome of the Donon. Dabo was a legendary centre of Celtic culture, later consecrated by the Gallo Romans for their worship of Belen, God of day and love. In its time it has held a temple dedicated to Mercury, a hunting lodge of King Dagobert, a feudal château, destroyed by order of Louis XIV in 1679, a humble chapel of homage to Léon IX (1002-54) (a local boy, born at Dabo, who became the great Pope reformer), and lastly by a sanctuary (1890). In its shadow lies the village, designed in the shape of a cross, that of St André. Its church (1763) tells the story of St León and St Blaise in its beautiful stained-glass windows.

Lunch at Dabo.

Wangenbourg

Continue along the twisting D45 and D218 through forests and meadows to Wangenbourg, a summer resort, prettily sited and overlooked by the Schneeberg. It also has a castle (13th to 14th century) which was destroyed by Swedish troops in 1663. Its five-sided keep and part of the walls still remain.

From Wangenbourg, continue south by D218 through the leafy forest of the Mossig. At 500m you will begin to descend via twisting roads towards Oberhaslach. The ruined castle of Nideck and its waterfalls appear. Alas, not much remains of this most romantically-sited fortress, burned down in 1636. But from its 13th-century tower and 14th-century keep there is a fine view over the forest and the Bruche valley, one of the most attractive parts of Alsace. From the belvédère further along the road there is a beautiful view of the castle, the valley and the rocks below.

Pilgrimages are still made to Oberhaslach further on, every November. Its chapel, restored in 1968, commemorates the time when 7th-century St Florent, protector of animals both wild and tame, lived here as a hermit before he became Bishop of Strasbourg.

Lovers of beautiful buildings should next take the D75 and N4 to Marmoutier, whose Bénédictine monastery, founded in the 6th century by St Leonard, disciple of Irish St Colomba, is reckoned to be one of the best examples of Roman architecture in Alsace. Marmoutier was named after the reformer, Abbot Maur. It was a favourite resting-place for kings and soon became well-known. The most visually pleasing part is its greyish-pink facade (c1150), comprising belfry and towers, which rise above a plain solid-looking front, pierced by tiny windows. Inside are beautiful Louis XV period wooden stalls and an 18th-century Sibermann organ. Concerts are now held here.

Return to Saverne for another night's stay.

DABO: USEFUL INFORMATION	
Tourist Office:	Place Eglise
	Tel: (87) 07 47 51
Population:	2,946
Interest:	Good views from the Rock of Dabo

Sarl Belle-Vue
57850 Dabo
Tel: (87) 07 40 21

A very cosy hotel with a view over the surrounding hills and forests.

Closed:	12-31 December and Tuesdays
Rooms:	15
Credit cards:	Euro, Visa, Carte Bleu
Food:	Regional dishes cooked by the patron chef
Rating:	★★★

DAY 5

Saverne, Marlenheim, Obernai: 38 km (24 miles)

Leave Saverne and head southwards to Marlenheim where an early lunch is recommended before a long, leisurely afternoon following the first part of the Route du Vin d'Alsace. On this picturesque drive, where the vineyards lie on the foothills and slopes of the Vosges, there are plenty of opportunities to taste some of the best wines of the region. The drive ends at Obernai, a picturesque and friendly town.

Overnight at Obernai.

Map references

Saverne	7°22′E 48°45′N
Wasselonne	7°27′E 48°38′N
Marlenheim	7°29′E 48°37′N
Molsheim	7°30′E 48°32′N
Rosheim	7°28′E 48°30′N
Obernai	7°29′E 48°28′N

Route shown p. 46.

Breakfast at Saverne.

From Saverne take the N4 past Wasselonne which is another old fortified town (one gateway remains), dominated by the ruins of its once strong castle and renowned for its August fair. Then on to Marlenheim for an early lunch at the traditional starting point of the wine road.

Lunch at Marlenheim.

Tour of Vosges and Wine Road

There are three attractive routes you can take south from Strasbourg to Colmar. Firstly, there is the Rhine road, starting with the D468 which runs through the plain of Alsace, lying on the region's east side, bounded by the Rhine. The countryside is fairly varied — large and small farms, villages and towns. Its fertility has made it a land of good fare, especially noted for fish dishes (fried or stewed) accompanied by white Alsatian wines.

Better still, there is the famous wine route, which runs through picturesque hamlets, villages and small towns, along the foothills of the Vosges, and is confined chiefly to the narrow band of terraced land between Marlenheim and Thann (184 kms). The Route du Vin d'Alsace is clearly signposted and many producers invite you to taste in their cellars without prior booking. There are also flower-decked roadside stalls displaying the wines and offering samples. The seven major Alsace wines — Appellation d'Origine Contrôlée — are all located along the Route: Sylvaner, Riesling, Gewurztraminer, Muscat d'Alsace, Tokay Pinot Gris, Klevner (also known as Pinot Blanc) and Pinot Noir (the only red). For further details see pp. 28-9.

Or, equally attractive, there is the mountain road through the Vosges massif.

Probably the best choice is a compromise as we did during a tour of the region, and combine the Vosges and wine route. Thus, one can vary long stretches of vineyards and delightful old towns with spectacular mountain scenery.

Molsheim

Start with D422 and the wine route to Molsheim. Lying on the Bruche River this is a picturesque old university town, at the foot of vine-clad hills, which produces Riesling. It was one of the ten cities of the Décapole (see p. 16).

To note especially here is its central square with fountain. Visit the Metzig, a typical 16th-century Rhenish Renaissance-style building, built by the Butchers' Guild, who held their meetings and sold their meat there. It has decorated gables, a balcony and is surmounted by a belfry. Here two angels strike the hour. It now holds a small museum, and wine-tasting takes place on the ground floor.

You can drive direct from here to Obernai, D422.

Detour
You can visit Rosheim (D422, D35), a Romanesque village lying in a leafy valley. The grey stone buildings in rue Général du Gaulle are supposed to be the oldest houses in Alsace. The most ancient one, known as the House of the Heathen, dates from 1170. Rosheim's gateway still stands, also some of the ramparts. There is an interesting 12th-century Rhenish-style church St Pierre and St Paul, built in greyish yellow stone. One of Alsace's few red wines is produced here. Return to the D422 and continue into Obernai.

Obernai

Obernai, another of the ten towns of the Décapole, is a real film set piece for tourists but charming nevertheless. I recommend you use the car parks on the outskirts of town — the ones in the centre get rather full. It still has its ramparts and one can make one's way past old houses and through narrow streets to Place du Marché, a large square surrounded by colourful medieval houses. There is a strong tradition in Obernai to fill the windowboxes with red geraniums; in season the old timbered houses are a blaze of colour. Place d'Etoile nearby is also picturesque. The town's main attraction is its 15th- to 16th-century Town Hall (restored in the 19th) particularly its balcony and 13th-century watch tower and 6-buckets' well. An ornate fountain (1903), surmounted by a statue of Ste Odile, patron saint of Alsace, stands in the centre of Place du Marché. The town is situated at the foot of Mont-Ste-Odile.

As Obernai was her birthplace, and we shall visit her convent tomorrow, I will insert her story here.

Odile, the daughter of Alderic or Etichon, a fierce 7th-century Duke of Alsace, was born blind and weakly. Her disappointed and angry father ordered that she be put to death. However, unknown to the Duke, her devoted nurse managed to hide the sickly child. Years passed. Odile was baptised and grew into a beautiful young woman. When her mother and brother eventually revealed her existence to the Duke, instead of pardoning them for disobeying his order, he flew into a rage and killed his son with his bare hands. He was then tortured by remorse. He believed he could redeem himself if he took Odile back and married her off to a knight. But Odile had other ideas. She resisted his orders and fled. It seemed that her irate father would commit yet another crime as he angrily pursued her. But Odile was saved by a miracle. Just as it seemed that she would be caught, a rock in the hills split open, allowing her to pass inside, then closed behind her, so that Etichon could not follow. He had to accept that his once despised daughter had a vocation. In recompense, he gave her his castle at Hohenbourg, where the convent of Ste Odile now stands.

Dinner and overnight at Obernai.

OBERNAI: USEFUL INFORMATION	
Tourist Office:	Chapelle du Beffroi
	Tel: (88) 95 64 13
Population:	9,444
Interest:	Traditional architecture and market place.

Hostellerie du Cerf
30 Rue du Général de Gaulle
67520 Marlenheim
Tel: (88) 87 73 73

The chef, Michel Husser, insists on fresh vegetables grown in the hotel garden. The food reflects this attention to quality. The building was originally a coaching inn. Now covered in a mass of flowers, there is a pretty courtyard to eat in as well as the beautifully beamed dining room.

Closed	Open all year, but restaurant shut Tuesdays and Wednesdays.
Rooms:	18
Credit cards:	Carte Bleu
Food:	Quite elaborate dishes with interesting use of vegetables and herbs e.g. Mille-Feuille de Beouf aux Champignons et confiture d'Oignon
Rating:	★★★★

Hôtel Le Parc
169 Rue Général Gourand
67210 Obernai
Tel: (88) 95 50 08

This hotel, established in 1954, is very proud of the many celebrities who have stayed here, and indeed continue to do so. This is probably one of the smartest hotels in the area, with prices to match. They aim for a country house atmosphere with all modern amenities and comforts. A chance to pamper yourself.

Closed:	Open all year
Rooms:	50
Facilities:	Swimming pool, sauna, jacuzzi, tennis courts, gardens
Credit cards:	Am.Ex, Mastercard, Visa
Food:	Try Cotelette de Saumon Fumée sur Choucroute
Rating:	★★★★

Hôtel Vosges
5 Place de la Gare
67210 Obernai
Tel: (88) 95 53 78

A charming small hotel. Your host Denis Weller is both Chef and Proprietor. He is keen on Alsatian specialities and offers guests a surprise gourmet buffet.

Closed:	Sunday evenings and Mondays
Rooms:	20
Facilities:	Parking, televisions and telephones in rooms
Credit cards:	Euro, Carte Bleu
Food:	Game and fish dishes a speciality
Rating:	★★

Storks' nest, Ostheim

DAY 6

Obernai, Le Hohwald, Ribeauvillé: 86 km (54 miles)

Leaving Obernai and, for the middle of the day, the wine route, zig-zag up through the western hills of the Vosges for lunch at Le Hohwald and on to the grandiose restored fortress of Haut-Koenigsbourg above Sélestat, before arriving for the night at Ribeauvillé — a delightful setting for further wine tasting.

Overnight at Ribeauvillé.

Map references

Obernai	7°29'E 48°28'N
Mont-Ste-Odile	7°25'E 48°27'N
Le Hohwald	7°20'E 48°25'N
Champ du Feu	7°16'E 48°24'N
St Martin	7°17'E 48°21'N
Villé	7°18'E 48°21'N
Châtenois	7°25'E 48°16'N
Haut-Koenigsbourg Castle	7°21'E 48°15'N
Sélestat	7°27'E 48°16'N
Ostheim	7°23'E 48°09'N
Ribeauvillé	7°19'E 48°11'N

Route shown pp. 82-3.

Breakfast at Obernai.

Mont-Ste-Odile

From Obernai, drive up the twisting roads to Mont-Ste-Odile (764 metres) on its promontory amid fir forests. Pilgrims still come to pray at the convent which was once an important cultural centre. Over the centuries, the convent has been burned down and rebuilt about ten times. We found it disappointingly commercialized. Also the views from its terrace, supposedly one of the best in Alsace, were shrouded in mist during our visit.

The group of buildings — 12-century Ste-Odile chapel (her tomb is inside), 11th-century Ste Croix chapel, the church and convent buildings (fairly recently restored) — stand within a 10 km perimeter, surrounded by the pagan wall, a series of stone blocks, a relic of the time when it was a place of refuge for Celtic and German tribes.

Le Hohwald

Continue between beech and fir woods (D426) to Le Hohwald, a small summer and winter sports' resort. Nearby is Champ du Feu, renowned for its waterfall and good viewpoint over the Vosges, the plain of Alsace and the Black Forest. A good spot to walk around before lunching at Le Hohwald.

Lunch at Le Hohwald.

On the winding D425, you first reach St Martin, then take D424 to Villé, noted for its liqueurs (raspberry and kirsch) and follow the road along the Giessen valley, passing Châtenois (13th-century church, vestiges of the town ramparts, a 13th-century château) towards Sélestat (N59), and catch your first glimpse of Haut-Koenigsbourg castle, an eagle's eyrie, on its 757 metres perch, dominating the Rhine plain.

Haut-Koenigsbourg Castle

This 15th-century castle, burned down by the Swedes during the Thirty Years' War, was Alsace's most magnificent ruin up to 1901.

It is worth a diversion (get on to D159 and 1 Bis, and drive about 1 km upwards) to visit this grandiose fortress in reddish-pink stone, complete with towers, turrets and ramparts, a frowning presence set amongst trees.

Its summit was first noted in a deed of Charlemagne's, 774, when it was called Stophanberch. For a time it was the property of the church, but in 1114 it was seized by the Duke of Swabia and Alsatian Frederick II. It was given to the counts of Wend, sold and battled over. It belonged to a Swiss family before it was burned by the Swedes. When it eventually came into the hands of the town of Sélestat, they could not afford to restore it, so they gave it to Kaiser Wilhelm II, who used historians and the best architects available to bring it back to its 15th-century magnificence. Its rooms are filled with the paraphernalia of the past. The Kaiser often stayed here.

Should you visit here, a word of advice. It is very popular so try and avoid the guided tours which are in very long-winded, highly-detailed French anyway, and slip in between them, so that you have more time to go round the rooms on your own. Once stuck in the crowd it is difficult to escape and you are trapped until the end of a quite lengthy tour.

Over the chimney piece in Salle des Fêtes is an inscription supposedly made on the Kaiser's last visit here in 1918 when World War One was going badly for him 'Das habe ich nicht Gewolt' (I didn't wish for this). I could not see it among the sea of heads, but you may be luckier. The guide books says its there. There is a grand view from the main tower over the countryside.

Sélestat

Sélestat, beside the Ill, an old town — its name is thought to have come from Schletto, a giant, who supposedly founded the town. It was once one of the most important cities of the Décapole and was a centre of Humanist thought in the mid-15th-century. It possesses a library quite unique in Europe. It became French during the 17th century when it played a part in France's line of defence. Many of the houses date from this time. Although a large part of the town was liberated by the Americans in December 1944, the front line was stabilised and the Germans dug in in the north-east suburbs for two months, causing considerable damage. Even so, it makes a good stopping place. There are a few old buildings to see although much of it is now a modern spread of houses and textile and chemical works.

If you park your car in the car park off Boulevard du Général Le Clerc, you can collect a map and booklet from the Information Office there. You are also very close to the old part of the town and the main buildings to see. You could have a quick snack at the Confiserie Tea Room, Salon de Thé Pâtisserie (good ice creams here).

Visit 12th-century Ste Foy, a red-grey building, plain inside and out, which succeeded an older building, which was part of a Bénédictine priory. The oldest part of the church is in the crypt and is also very plain.

Leave the church from the door at the side and continue to St Georges, 13th- to 15th-century, but considerably restored, and a cathedral. It is still in the pinkish grey stone, but perhaps a more muted shade. Note the coloured statues of biblical figures and the more recent marble ones. Some of the stained-glass windows are interesting. It has a highly-decorated pulpit. For a curiosity, look at the ugly face on the second pillar on the left, going down the nave. It represents St Barthélemy, patron saint of butchers.

After St Georges, turn down rue de Sel towards the Bibliothéque Humaniste. This can be visited: weekdays 9 to 12, 13 to 17; Saturdays, 9 to 12. It was founded in 1452 when Sélestat had a famous university. Both Erasmus and Bucer attended the college here. Its centre was this private library (some 2000 books) which belonged to Beatus Rhenanus, friend of Erasmus.

Follow the N83 south to Ostheim, 'the martyred city'. All that remains of the town obliterated by the Second World War is one wall — on the top of which is a nest of storks, the symbol of Alsace. Take the D416 to Ribeauvillé.

Ribeauvillé

At Ribeauvillé, our next stop, one can sample during the evening the best Traminer and Reisling of the region. This charming old town and resort is good viewed on foot. Its main square with its Renaissance-style greyish-red stone fountain and Butchers' Tower at one end (this separated the high town from the low, or the old 13th-century one from the newer 16th-century one) is particularly attractive.

Ribeauvillé was once the home of the Counts of Ribeaupierre, one of the most powerful families in the region up to the 19th century, and the town is overlooked by three castles, the ruined Haut Ribeaupierre, Girsberg and St Ulrich (a one-time luxurious living-place of the Counts of Ribeaupierre).

Ribeauvillé is renowned for one of the most celebrated festivals in Alsace (last Sunday in August), the Pfiffertag, the day of the strolling players. In medieval times, strolling fiddlers came to the town to pay homage to their lord, the sire of Ribeaupierre and our Lady of Dussenach (Notre-Dame de Dussenach is a nearby convent and place of pilgrimage). Today this popular festival involves choirs, historical processions, brass-bands and country-dancing. There is also free wine-tasting at the wine fountain in Place Hôtel de Ville.

Dinner and overnight at Ribeauvillé.

VILLE: USEFUL INFORMATION

Tourist Office:	à la Mairie
	Tel: (88) 57 11 57
Population:	1616

RIBEAUVILLE: USEFUL INFORMATION

Tourist Office:	1 Grand Rue
	Tel: (89) 73 62 22
Population:	4611
Interest:	Centre for renaturalising storks at Hunawihr (3 km)

La Petite Auberge

26 Rue Principale
67140 Le Hohwald
Tel: (88) 08 33 05

A fine little hostel run by M. and Mme. Robert Hubrecht. In the beamed dining room you can eat a menu of the house specialities — game, fish and choucroute.

Closed:	Wednesdays and Thursdays
Credit cards:	Euro, Mastercard, Carte Bleu
Food:	Alsatian dishes
Rating:	★★

Hôtel Restaurant Les Vosges

2 Grand Rue
68150 Ribeauvillé
Tel: (89) 73 61 39

A medium sized hotel with a charming town house exterior but very modern interior decor. You can choose a room according to your purse, likewise your meal in the restaurant.

Closed:	1 February to 3 March and Mondays
Rooms:	20
Facilities:	Telephones and televisions in rooms
Credit cards:	Am.Ex, Euro, Carte Bleu
Food:	Fish and game
Rating:	★★★

Hôtel Restaurant Le Cheval Blanc

122 Grand Rue
68150 Ribeauvillé
Tel: (89) 73 61 38

Closed:	December to February and Mondays
Rooms:	25
Credit cards:	Euro, Visa
Rating:	★★

DAY 7

Ribeauvillé, Kaysersberg, Colmar: 26 km (16 miles)

After spending the morning at 16th-century Riquewihr and the splendid wine town of Kaysersberg, continue into Colmar for lunch and devote the afternoon to exploring the town. At this point the itinerary leaves the wine route to begin the journey eastwards tomorrow into Lorraine. If you have extra time you could travel the rest of the wine route to Thann near Mulhouse.

Overnight at Colmar.

Map references

Ribeauvillé	7°19'E 48°11'N
Riquewihr	7°18'E 48°10'N
Kaysersberg	7°16'E 48°08'N
Colmar	7°22'E 48°05'N
Orbey	7°10'E 48°08'N
Les Trois Epis	7°13'E 48°06'N
Turckheim	7°17'E 48°05'N
Mulhouse	7°20'E 47°45'N
Thann	7°05'E 47°49'N
Cernay	7°10'E 47°48'N

Route shown pp. 82-3.

Breakfast at Ribeauvillé.

South from Ribeauvillé (D1b) past Hunawihr, where they are striving to reintroduce the stork population, lies (D3) Riquewihr.

Riquewihr

If Ribeauvillé is an extremely attractive and quaint old town, Riquewihr is even more so. We approached it along twisting roads, through stretches of golden vineyards, which covered the surrounding wayside hills.

Riquewihr is really another medieval film-set town, a tourist trap, but still delightful. It has been miraculously preserved and is a living museum of a fortified 16th-century wine town.

Leave your car outside — you will have to anyway: there is no traffic inside the old town. You will make your way through old gateways and find yourself mounting the cobbled streetway, past timber-framed blue, pink and buff-washed buildings, decorated with lanterns, inn signs and boxes of flowers, possibly trying to resist the many invitations to descend to cellars and sample the local wine. At the top is a fountain — at festival time, I believe it runs with wine — and the Doldergate (1291) with a house perched on top. Narrow streets, arched and equally picturesque, run off the main one. Occasionally a head pokes out of a house window to survey the tourist army below. What must it be like to actually *live* in this Hansel and Gretel town with strangers continually tramping your streets? I suppose its alright if you own a shop, tavern, hotel, restaurant or cafe here.

Riquewihr always managed to maintain its independence. It is said they softened up intending invaders with wine. You can spend hours here wandering up and down the old streets. There are some small museums and a pale pink Protestant church, very plain and clean, to see.

Take the D3, D28 to Kaysersberg.

Kaysersberg

We spent a night in Kaysersberg, another old fortified wine town, but larger than Riquewihr, and with a very pretty bridge (15th- to 16th-century), situated amid old houses.

Kaysersberg translates to mean 'Emperor's Hill'. In Caesar's time, it commanded one of the most important passages between Gaul and the valley of the Rhine. During the course of time, it continued to justify its title, as it was acquired in the 13th century by the Emperor Frederick II, who fortified the town and castle against possible invasion by the Duke of Lorraine.

It possesses a 12th-century church (fine reredos, carved in wood by Jean Bongartz of Colmar, 1518). The chapel behind is built on two tiers. the underneath one has been turned into an ossuary — I was amazed to glimpse the stacks of bones through its window.

Doctor Schweitzer was born in the town. His house contains a museum dedicated to him.

Leave Kaysersberg via N415 to Colmar. The road passes Ammeschwihr, lying between vineyards, and particularly noted for its fine wines. The town was badly damaged during the battle of the Colmar pocket in the last war, but has been rebuilt in the pretty Alsatian style. Continue into Colmar.

Detour

You could make a side trip to Orbey, Les Trois Epis and Turckheim. Take the N415 northwest out of Kaysersberg, and then the D48 to Orbey, a peaceful stopover and a good centre for walks. Next Les Trois Epis, D11, (the three ears of wheat), a health resort and completely rebuilt after the last war. Like Orbey, it makes a good centre for exploring the neighbourhood on foot or by car.

Continue on the D11 to Turckheim, another picturesque old village, triangular in shape and surrounded by a wall, and just delightful to wander round. Its most splendid old house is the Hôtel Deux Clefs (1620), an 'olde worlde' inn. Place Turenne, surrounded by old houses, was named after Vicomte de Turenne (1611-1675), one of the great captains of history, to commemorate his famous victory when in 1674 he forced the Imperial army, which threatened Alsace, to retreat across the Rhine. Napoleon, a warm admirer of his tactics, advised his generals to read and reread about his campaigns. Interestingly enough, Napoleon drew many of his generals from the Alsace region.

In summer, a Town Crier, complete with lantern, halberd and three-cornered hat, performs at dusk in the town.

D11, via Niedermorschwihr to Colmar.

Colmar

Lunch at Colmar.

Colmar's chief charm lies in the Alsatian character of its medieval and early Renaissance houses and streets.

Colmar started as a Frankish royal residence beside the Lauch, a villa in which Charlemagne and his son, Louis the Debonair, often stayed. Around it grew a small village of artisans. A tower (Colombier) standing there, a symbol of power and nobility which harboured a dovecot, was eventually to give its name to the future city. Villa Columbria, the house of doves, became Columbaria, Columbra and finally Colmar.

Colmar, which managed to obtain a charter in the 13th century became one of the ten towns of the Décapole. It always remained pro-French in spite of its long union with Germany after the Franco-Prussian war. During the last war, French and American troops attacking the town from the north and south, finally closed the 'Colmar pocket' on February 9th, 1945, and the Germans were pushed out of Alsace.

Some houses to particularly note in Colmar are the Maison Pfitzer — a graceful wooden arcade dates from 1537 — and opposite it, Maison Schongauer, home of the painter and decorated with carved wooden heads in the rue des Marchands; and the Maison des Têtes, whose facade is richly decorated with carved heads and which is now a restaurant in rue des Têtes.

The Musée d'Unterlinden occupies the site of an old convent dating from the 13th century and which was founded by two widows. It first came under the rule of St Augustin, then the order of St Dominique. It was dispersed during the Revolution. To see there especially is the world-famous 16th-century Issenheim altarpiece 'The Great Crucifixion' by Mathias Gothardt-Nithardt (better known as Mathias Grunewald).

Colmar's old custom-house dates from the 15th century when the wine trade was flourishing. 13th- to 14th-century St Martin's church (usually called the Cathedral) has some interesting wood carvings around the choir, and sculpture around the west and south doorways. Also, don't miss a visit to 'Little Venice' (restored tanners' quarters, and canal-laced quay), which can be viewed from St Peter's bridge, over the Lauch, which crosses Boulevard St Pierre, to the south-east of town.

A wine fair is held here in August and a Fête de la Choucroute in September. Colmar also makes a good excursion centre for the wine route, which continues on past delectable old towns and villages to Thann (noted for collegiate church, St Thiébaut, locally called the cathedral, and one of the finest in Alsace); and for journeys into the higher reaches of the Vosges. Eastwards lies Germany, southwards Mulhouse, N422.

Detour

After Strasbourg, Mulhouse, crossed by the Ill and the Canal de Rhône au Rhin, is Alsace's most industrial and prosperous city. Although not picturesque it is neat, sober and progressive. A city since 803 AD when part of the Germanic Holy Roman Empire, it gained its freedom in the 14th century, joined the Décapole, then became a member of the Swiss Federation for about 300 years. After entering France in 1798, its history has followed that of the rest of Alsace.

Mulhouse's industrial growth dates from the middle of the 18th century, when three of her citizens, Samuel Koechlin, J.J. Schmaltzer and J.H. Dollfus founded a mill which printed cottons (imitations of Indian prints). Their popularity and success encouraged the establishment of other industries, such as linen, fabrics, dyes, then chemical products and metallurgy. The discovery of potash nearby made this town, and France, one of the world's most important sources of this ore.

There is not very much here of interest to tourists, apart from the 16th-century Town Hall (Rhineland Renaissance) and its historical museum; the museum of printed fabrics, very well displayed; the museum of fine arts, and zoo and Botanical Gardens in the south east of the town.

Mulhouse is a good centre for excursions in Alsace, the Vosges, Jura, Black Forest and Switzerland.

If you have a few extra days you could take the N422/A35 direct to Mulhouse, and return to Colmar via the lower end of the wine route — N66 to Thann, D35 to Cernay, N83 back to Colmar.

Overnight at Colmar.

Maison des Têtes
19 rue des Têtes
68000 Colmar
Tel: (89) 29 43 43

A beautiful ornate old building, built in 1609, offers a variety of ambiances to eat in. From the ground floor restaurant with stained glass windows and wood panelling to an internal courtyard shaded by a venerable vine.

Closed:	15 January to 15 February, Sunday evenings and Mondays
Credit cards:	Am.Ex, Diners, Euro, Carte Bleu
Food:	Imaginative regional cooking
Rating:	★★★

Les Hortensias
6 rue Henner
Colmar
Tel: (89) 41 44 89

Closed:	5 August to 2 September, 2 to 13 January, Saturdays and Sundays
Credit cards:	Am.Ex, Euro, Diners, Visa
Food:	Fish and seafood a speciality
Rating:	★★★

Hôtel Bristol
Place de la Gare
68025 Colmar
Tel: (89) 23 59 59

An imposing looking exterior with an elegant and luxurious inside. The hotel has a top class restaurant attached, Le Rendezvous de Chasse. The 7-course menu degustation is particularly notable.

Closed:	Open all year
Rooms:	70
Facilities:	Minibars, telephones in rooms
Credit cards:	Am.Ex, Diners, Mastercard, Visa
Food:	Very elegant, try their Turbot aux deux celeris.
Rating:	★★★★

COLMAR: USEFUL INFORMATION

Tourist Office:	4 rue Unterlinden
	Tel: (89) 41 02 29
Population:	63,764
Facilities:	Airport
Interest:	Architecture and churches

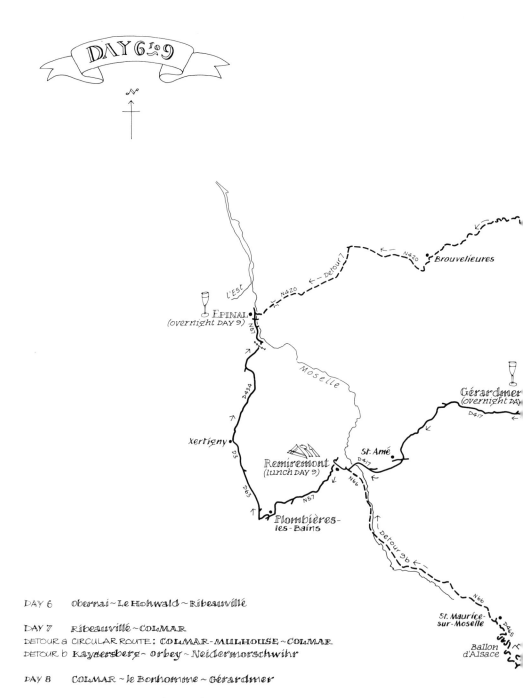

DAY 6 to 9

Brouvelieures

L'Est

EPINAL
(overnight DAY 9)

Moselle

Gérardmer
(overnight DAY

Xertigny

Remiremont
(lunch DAY 9)

St. Amé

Plombières-
les-Bains

St. Maurice-
sur-Moselle

Ballon
d'Alsace

N420

N420

Detour 7

N57

D434

D3

D63

N57

N66

D417

D417

N66

Detour 9b

DAY 6   Obernai ~ Le Hohwald ~ Ribeauvillé

DAY 7   Ribeauvillé ~ COLMAR
DETOUR a CIRCULAR ROUTE : COLMAR ~ MULHOUSE ~ COLMAR
DETOUR b Kaysersberg ~ Orbey ~ Neidermorschwihr

DAY 8   COLMAR ~ le Bonhomme ~ Gérardmer

DAY 9   Gérardmer ~ Remiremont ~ EPINAL
DETOUR a Gérardmer ~ St. Dié ~ EPINAL
DETOUR b Gérardmer ~ Thann ~ Remiremont

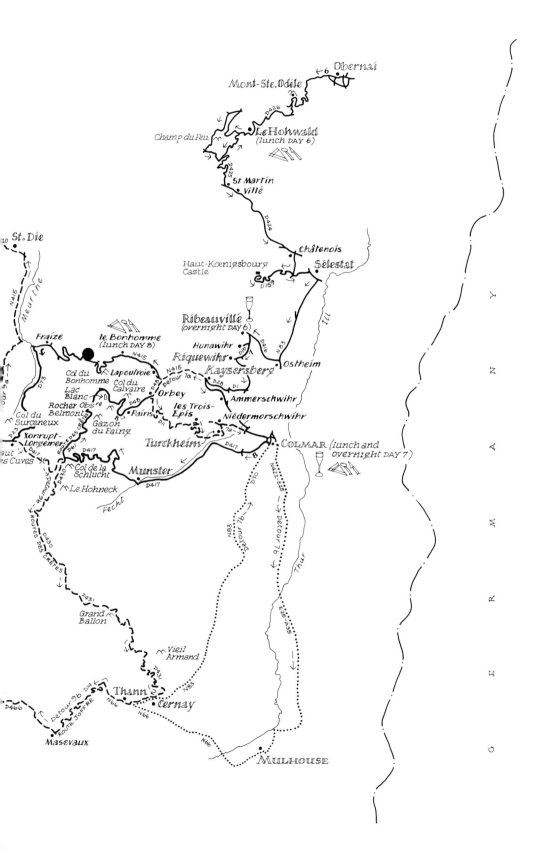

Gérardmer

DAY 8

Colmar, Munster, Le Bonhomme, Gérardmer: 110 km, (69 miles)

Leaving Colmar the route begins the crossing of the southern Vosges. The scenery is wilder and higher than in the north — water crashes in torrents through ancient glacial valleys. Lunch is at Le Bonhomme and the day ends at Gérardmer, set in the mountains amid forests by a magnificent lake.

Overnight at Gérardmer.

Map references

Colmar	7°22'E 48°05'N
Munster	7°08'E 48°03'N
Col de la Schlucht	7°02'E 48°04'N
Le Hohneck	7°02'E 48°02'N
Col du Calvaire	7°05'E 48°08'N
Gazon du Fang	7°05'E 48°06'N
Rocher Obs Belmont	7°06'E 48°07'N
Lac Blanc	7°05'E 48°08'N
Pairis	7°07'E 48°06'N
Lapoutroie	7°10'E 48°09'N
Le Bonhomme	7°06'E 48°11'N
Col du Bonhomme	7°05'E 48°09'N
Fraize	7°00'E 48°12'N
Col du Surceneux	6°57'E 48°06'N
Xonrupt-Longemer	6°55'E 48°05'N
Gérardmer	6°53'E 48°04'N

Route shown p. 82-3.

Breakfast at Colmar.

Not only do the grey-granite hills of the southern Vosges rise higher than those of the northern but they are more uniform in shape. Above the tree-line, open pastures (chaumes) cover the rounded tops (ballons), where once bison, oxen, deer and even wild horses were supposed to have roamed. Today, in summer, flocks with tinkling bells range the springy turf: in winter it is a playground for skiers.

Munster

We drive to Munster via the valley of the Fecht, at first broad, then narrowing as it gradually rises. Irish monks came to Munster in the 7th century to found an abbey, which gave its name Munster (Monastère) to the town. Munster, along with nine neighbouring villages, eventually became a part of the Décapole. Today this rather grey town is a spa and is noted for its textile industry, also a hard rather smelly cheese. You can do a tour of the Route des Fromages, which takes in 'fermes auberges', which serve local dishes (June to October). Munster is also a good starting place for a tour of the valley of Munster and the Route des Crêtes, a ridge road running along the highest part of the Vosges, between the Col du Bonhomme and Thann (83 kms). It was built by the French high command in World War One and offers some of the best views over the region.

From Munster our route follows the D417. Col de la Schlucht (1139 metres), is a summer and winter sports' resort and famous beauty spot on the crest road from which there are some fine views over the Munster valley and Hohneck slopes. If you take the D430 south out of Col de la Schlucht, there is a track on the left which allows you to drive to the summit of Le Hohneck. There is a hotel at the top of the track. A short walk to the actual summit — marked by an orientation table — and you have sensational views over the Vosges, sometimes even as far as the Alps. This is an excellent way to get a clear picture of the landscape you are travelling through. Although, obviously, it is only worth doing when the weather is clear.

Return to Col de la Schlucht, and you can meander through the range, following the Crest Road, the D61 to Col du Calvaire, then D48 II/D48 to Orbey (on yesterday's detour) passing Gazon du Faing (1303 metres), Rocher Obs Belmont (1272 metres), Lac Blanc (this large lake is linked to Lac Noir by underground pipes; turbines create power for the region) and Pairis (its abbey, destroyed during the Revolution, was once a place of pilgrimage; its monks had a reputation for saintliness and wisdom). Then the D48, passing Lapoutroie, and the N415 to Le Bonhomme.

Lunch at Le Bonhomme.

On my visit to Col du Bonhomme, a little after the town, a thick mist was suspended over the valley below like a floating veil. The 'chaumes' around us, mantled by very soft grass, berries and heather, glowed brown, mauve, green and yellow, against a brilliant blue sky. It was not too difficult to imagine them covered in snow with skiers gliding down their gentle slopes. We descended along sinuous roads (N415) to Fraize.

Then travel down the valley of the little Meurthe (D73) to Col du Surceneux (D23) towards Xonrupt-Longemer and the D417, passing Saut des Cuves, where torrents crash in foaming cascades amid granite rocks, to Gérardmer.

Gérardmer

This winter sports' centre and summer resort lies besides the largest lake in a region of lakes. Unfortunately, although so beautifully situated, Gérardmer was badly damaged in the last war. The Germans burned down the town a few days before it was liberated on Sunday, 19th November, 1944. It appears now as a modern town, not particularly remarkable, but pleasant enough.

Gérardmer is officially classified as a health resort due to the purity of the mountain air and the water which is said to have many beneficial properties. The lake offers a full range of water sports but perhaps the best activity after a day's driving is to take a walk on the surrounding hill slopes. Every spring these slopes are carpeted with daffodils. Millions are picked by the local children for the annual spring Festival of Daffodils. (It is a large celebration and for the procession each float can contain up to 200,000 blooms.)

Gérardmer makes a good stopping place as there are plenty of hotels, and it is a good excursion centre — for the region and for Germany and Switzerland. Interestingly, the surrounding area is one of the most important textile centres of the Vosges.

Overnight at Gérardmer.

Hôtel Restaurant de la Poste
68650 Le Bonhomme
Tel: (89) 47 51 10

A charming hostel nestling on the hillside of this little town. It has a distinct country air with its flowerboxes and window shutters. The restaurant continues the theme with its magnificent 'welsh' dresser and carved furniture. All the food is prepared by chef/patron, Arnand Toscani.

Closed:	18 November-25 December
Rooms:	21
Credit cards:	Am.Ex, Visa, Euro
Food:	Specialities include Terrine de Foie de Volaille, Canard à l'Orange and Baeckoffea
Rating:	★★

La Réserve
esplanade du Lac
Gérardmer
Tel: (26) 63 21 60

Overlooking the lake this hotel's spectacular position is also reflected in its cooking which is highly recommended.

Closed:	Mid-November to mid-December
Rooms:	32
Facilities:	Telephones and televisions in rooms, private parking
Credit cards:	Am.Ex, Diners, Visa, Euro
Food:	Try Escargots en cassolette or Jambon de Montagne braisé au vin d'Alsace
Rating:	★★★

Hôtel Viry et Restaurant l'Aubergade
Place Déportés
Gérardmer
Tel: (26) 63 02 41

Although situated in the centre of the town there are pleasant tables for eating outside.

Closed:	Wednesdays out of season
Rooms:	18
Facilities:	Television and telephones in rooms, parking
Credit cards:	Euro, Visa
Food:	Good cooking at very reasonable prices
Rating:	★★

GÉRARDMER: USEFUL INFORMATION

Tourist Office:	Place Déportés Tel: (29) 63 08 74
Population:	9,647
Facilities:	Winter sports, lake, casino

Remiremont

DAY 9

Gérardmer, Remiremont, Epinal: 68 km (42 miles)

Heading through the Vosges toward the Moselle valley, stop at Remiremont for lunch before visiting the famous spa of Plombières-les-Bains in the afternoon and then on to Epinal. Two optional routes on leaving Gérardmer are detailed, the first is to head for St Dié and then on to Epinal. The second longer option, winds through the highest peaks of the southern Vosges before joining the main route at Remiremont.

Overnight at Epinal.

Map references

Gérardmer	6°53′E 48°04′N
St Amé	6°41′E 48°02′N
Remiremont	6°35′E 48°02′N
Plombières-les-Bains	6°27′E 47°57′N
Epinal	6°26′E 48°11′N

Detour 1

St Dié	7°56′E 48°17′N

Detour 2

Le Markstein	7°02′E 47°55′N
Grand Ballon	7°06′E 47°54′N
Vieil Armand	7°10′E 47°52′N
Cernay	7°10′E 47°48′N
Masevaux	7°00′E 47°46′N
St Maurice-sur-Moselle	6°49′E 47°52′N

Route shown p. 82-3.

Breakfast at Gérardmer.

Before leaving here, it is pleasant to drive around the lake, a grand peaceful stretch of water, popular with campers, boaters, bathers and anglers.

Follow the D417 to St Amé and to Remiremont.

Remiremont

Remiremont, attractively set in the high valley of the Moselle, once the site of a famous convent, is now more celebrated for its industries and the production of confectionery.

At first, in the 7th century, a monastery was founded here at the confluence of the Moselle and the Moselotte, but later, during medieval times, this was replaced by a convent for gentlewomen, and the town grew up around it. To be accepted the nuns had to prove a noble ancestry on both sides for 200 years. This convent was unique in that the nuns took no vows of chastity and lived in houses rather than cells. Only the Abbess took any vows; the nuns owed allegiance only to the Pope. They became known as Dames, then Chanoinesses and lastly 'tantes' and novices as 'nieces'. They were popular locally: in fact the people here petitioned that their order not be suppressed by the Revolution, but to no avail.

There is little to remind you of their existence today except the objects contained in the Musée Charles Friry (situated in two old houses belonging to the Chanoinesses) and a local gingerbread called a 'Chanoiness'. Remiremont's main street, rue Général du Gaulle, has some arcaded shops dating from the 13th century.

Lunch at Remiremont.

Plombières-les-Bains

Take the N57 to Plombières-les-Bains, framed by trees, a well-known spa for digestive troubles and rheumatism. The waters were discovered over 2000 years ago by the Romans. The town lies in the picturesque Augronne valley. Most of the main town buildings are 18th and early 19th century. Some of its streets are named after famous invalids who spent time here.

Epinal

D63 and D434 to Epinal, situated at a crossroads, and the capital of the Vosges. The town, built on the two banks of the Moselle, has a number of parks and gardens, also an old quarter round Place des Vosges. Note the 11th-century Basilica St Maurice. During the 18th century, Epinal became famous for its coloured prints. At the Imagerie Pellerin you can see how they are made and purchase samples. At the museum of the Vosges department and International Museum of Imagery, there is a museum of prints, a collection of Gallo-Roman and medieval sculpture, also a very good art collection.

Overnight at Epinal.

Two detours you could make from Gérardmer.

Detour 1
Take the D8, N415 to St Dié, about a 30 kms drive, a tourist centre and small industrial town. Although it suffered badly in the last war — it was almost destroyed — it has been rebuilt around its red sandstone cathedral, a blend of Romanesque, Gothic and classical styles. The smaller church of Notre-Dame is a good example of Rhenish Romanesque. The town originally evolved around its Bénédictine priory, founded in the 7th century by Saint Déodat.

Perhaps St Dié's main claim to fame is that its *Cosmographiae Introductio* (1507) was the first geographical work to suggest and print the name America (after Amerigo Vespucci) for the New World. A copy of this publication is on display at the Public Library. St Dié was also the birthplace of Jules Ferry, the minister who had so much effect on French education. Also the first printing works in France was established here.

Take the N420 to Epinal (47 kms).

Detour 2

This trip is a long one and will take you to the southern end of the Route des Crêtes, passing the Vosges' highest peaks.

Take the D417 to the Col de la Schlucht, then on the Crest Road (D430/D431), where you will see the Hohneck (1362 metres), a famous beauty spot with tremendous views. On a clear day you can see the Alps. You will also pass Le

Markstein, resort and winter sports' centre, and Grand Ballon which at 1424 metres is the highest point in the Vosges. Again tremendous views from its top. All around here is the most dramatic part of the Route des Crêtes, comprising crests, precipices and overhangs and, of course, splendid views.

Vieil Armand, or Hartmannswillerkopf (956 metres), some 13 kms further on, was the scene of some terrible fighting in World War One. Something like 30,000 men were killed in this area.

After Cernay, last place on the Route des Crêtes, take the D35/N66 to Thann, a commercial centre at the foot of the Vosges. It claims that its church or 'cathedral' St Thiébaut, is the finest in Alsace.

Next follow the Route Joffre (D14 bIV), another beautiful road created by the army in the First World War and named after a famous general, which links the valleys of Doller and Thur to Masevaux, a small industrial and commercial town.

Then take the very twisting D466 past Ballon d'Alsace (1250 metres), and D465 to St Maurice-sur-Moselle and N66 to rejoin the main route at Remiremont.

Le Clos Huertebise
13 Chemin des Capuchins
88200 Remiremont
Tel: (29) 62 08 04

A 63-seat restaurant with several menus and several specialities among which are Tartare of Salmon wrapped in smoked salmon, poached sea bass with asparagus and a stew of quail marinated in fresh thyme.

Closed:	Sunday evenings and Mondays
Credit cards:	Carte Bleu
Rating:	★★★

```
REMIREMONT: USEFUL INFORMATION
Tourist Office:        2 place H-Utard
                       Tel: (29) 62 23 70
Population:            10,680
```

```
PLOMBIÈRES LES BAINS: USEFUL
INFORMATION
Tourist Office:        rue Stanislas
                       Tel: (29) 66 01 30
Population:            890
Facilities:            Spa, casino
```

Hôtel Ibis
quai Maréchal de Contades
Epinal
Tel: (29) 28 28

Closed:	Open all year
Rooms:	60
Facilities:	Garage and parking, lift and rooms for disabled people
Credit cards:	Euro, Visa
Food:	The restaurant is very reasonably priced
Rating:	★★

Hôtel Mercure
13 place E. Stein
Epinal
Tel: (29) 35 18 68

Closed:	Open all year
Rooms:	45
Facilities:	Parking, lifts, rooms available for disabled people
Credit cards:	Am.Ex, Diners, Euro, Visa
Food:	There is a restaurant called Le Mouton Blanc
Rating:	★★★★

Hôtel Azur
54 quai des Bon Enfants
Epinal
Tel: (29) 64 05 25

A small modest hotel overlooking a slipstream of the Moselle. It does not, however, take credit cards.

Closed:	Open all year
Rooms:	20
Facilities:	Telephones
Food:	No restaurant
Rating:	★★

There are two highly recommended restaurants in this town, which it would be a pity to miss. Both the food and their selection of regional wines are superb.

Les Abbesses
23 rue Louvière
Epinal
Tel: (29) 82 53 69

Closed:	3 to 17 January, 16 to 31 August, Sunday evenings and Mondays
Credit cards:	Am.Ex, Euro, Diners, Visa

Food: Try their Saucisson de foie gras
fumé or Sandre rôti aux écailles
de pommes de terre

Rating: ★★★★

Relais des Ducs de Lorraine
16 quai Colonel-Sérot
Epinal
Tel: (29) 34 39 87

Closed: 15 to 30 August, 1 to 8 March,
Sunday evenings and Mondays

Credit cards: Visa

Food: Again very high quality and
interesting. For instance their
speciality — Dos de Sandre au
gris de Toul

Rating: ★★★★

EPINAL: USEFUL INFORMATION

Tourist Office:	13 rue Comédie
	Tel: (29) 82 53 32
Population:	40,954
Interest:	Old town, museum and park

Fountain in Stanislas Place, Nancy

DAY 10

Epinal, Lunéville, Nancy: approx. 90 km (56 miles)

North from Epinal up the Moselle valley lies Lunéville on the Meurthe river. After visiting the famous château continue into Nancy for lunch, and the afternoon can be spent exploring the traditional capital of Lorraine. If you prefer spas to châteaux you could detour to renowned Vittel for lunch before heading into Nancy.

Overnight at Nancy.

Map references

Epinal	6°26'E 48°11'N
Charmes	6°18'E 48°23'N
Bayon	6°19'E 48°28'N
Lunéville	6°30'E 48°36'N
St Nicholas-de-Port	6°17'E 48°38'N
Nancy	6°10'E 48°42'N

Detour

Vittel	5°57'E 48°13'N
Contrexéville	5°54'E 48°12'N

Route shown pp. 108-9

Breakfast at Epinal.

Leave Epinal on the N57 to cross the canal at Charmes, then the D9/D112 to Bayon, D9/D914 to Lunéville.

Lunéville

Lunéville, a Versailles-type town is a mini Nancy, a foretaste of what is to come. Its celebrated château was built at the beginning of the 18th century by Duke Léopold, the last Duke of Lorraine, using the best artists and craftsmen of his time, such as architect Boffrand, pupil of Mansart, and ironwright, Jean Lamour. Stanislas, who later lived there, embellished and improved it. He surrounded himself with the artists and intellectuals of the day. Voltaire was one. He claimed that he found it difficult to believe that he had changed places when he went from Versailles to Lunéville. Artist Georges de la Tour lived at Lunéville from 1626 to 1652. Stanislas died here in 1776.

The château stands in the landscaped Parc des Bosquets (son et lumière performances are held here in summer), and houses a local museum, which has a fine collection of the 18th-century faïence for which the region is noted. Motor-bike buffs might care for a visit to M. Chapleur's motor bikes' museum near the château gates. Chapleur, who started his collection in the 1930s when working for Citroën, has amassed over 200 models — some of which are works of art of their period. You will see pushbikes dating from 1865. Lunéville, surrounded by forests, is a spacious town, which has managed to retain its gracious 18th-century atmosphere.

St Nicholas-de-Port

Take the N4 to Nancy via St Nicholas-de-Port, an industrial town, but still dominated by the lofty towers of its magnificent Flamboyant Gothic basilica (built 1494-1544). Knights from Lorraine returned from the Holy Land with a finger of St Nicholas. The church was built to house this holy relic, which became an important place of pilgrimage. Joan of Arc came to the 11th-century sanctuary, which preceded it, to pray to St Nicholas, a saint who was supposed to work miracles in the area and is now the protector of the basilica. Legend has it that St Nicholas brought back to life three boys who had been chopped up by a butcher.

Nancy

Nancy, old city of the Dukes, is Lorraine's historic capital. The city, about 1000 years old, may have taken its name from Nanceium. Some say it comes from the Chinese 'Nan Soy', which means 'difficult to destroy'. During the 11th century, a castle (replaced in the 13th) was erected between two marshes near the Meurthe. First a village, then a town, grew around what was to become the residence of the Dukes' government. When Duke René II defeated Charles the Rash, the last of Burgundy's great dukes, in the battle for Nancy in 1477, this great victory considerably enhanced Lorraine's prestige. Their rallying sign for the battle, the double cross of Lorraine (taken from Godefroy de Bouillon, famous crusader and founder of this line) became a symbol for Lorraine's resistance and patriotism.

The dukes developed their city. A new palace was created and Nancy was enlarged. A new town with straight-crossing streets was built to the south of the old town, leaving a wide space, an esplanade, between the two. Duke Charles II encouraged artisans to settle there, also clergymen. Thirteen monasteries were built during the next century. A souvenir of this era is the rue des Quatre Eglises.

Then came the calamities and destruction of the Thirty Years' War. After the Treaty of Ryswick, 1697, Duke Leopold of Lorraine did his best to restore the Duchy to its earlier prosperity.

His son, Duke François III, who left Nancy to become Emperor of Austria, through his marriage with Marie Thérèse of Austria in 1740, ceded his kingdom to Stanislas Leczinski, the dethroned King of Poland, and father-in-law of Louis XV, in exchange for Tuscany. The French king, his eyes very firmly fixed on Lorraine, insisted that the Duchy pass to France on Stanislas's death.

Stanislas, continuing Duke Leopold's work in restoring prosperity, set up steel, glassware and pottery industries. As a great patron of the arts, he spent much time and money turning Nancy into a beautiful and regal city. He wanted its proud citizens to see all that was best in French culture.

Stanislas appointed a Nancy architect, Emmanuel Héré. Ramparts were razed, old moats filled in, and a new quarter created to unite the old and new town. Héré's masterpiece was Nancy's main square. Its beautiful wrought-

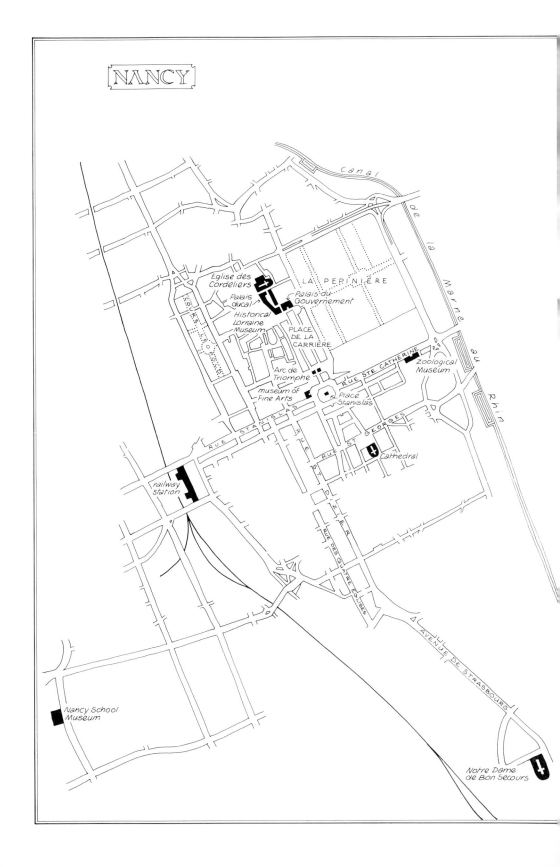

NANCY

Canal

le Marne au Rhin

Eglise des
Cordeliers

LA PÉPINIÈRE

Palais
ducal

Palais du
Gouvernement

Historical
Lorraine
Museum

PLACE
DE LA
CARRIÈRE

Arc de
Triomphe

RUE STE. CATHERINE

Zoological
Museum

museum of
Fine Arts

Place
Stanislas

RUE STANISLAS

RUE ST GEORGES

RUE DE 10 ZIÈR

Cathedral

railway
station

RUE DES QUATRE EGLISES

AVENUE DE STRASBOURG

Nancy School
Museum

Notre Dame
de Bon Secours

iron railings, gates painted in maroon and gold, embellished by that master of ironwork, Jean Lamour, and impressive monuments and fountains are reminiscent of Versailles.

Lanterns adorn the square like jewellery. At night when lit and sparkling, the effect is quite magical. Named Place Royale, a statue of Louis XV was first placed in its centre. An Arc de Triomphe, also erected in honour of this monarch, leads from it into Place de La Carrière (an old jousting place). At its end and facing the Arc de Triomphe, is the Palais du Gouvernment, the old residence of the governors of Lorraine.

Stanislas completed the city's embellishments by creating the Pepinière, a fine promenade which harmonises with the monuments and nearby squares. Today it contains a tree-nursery, rose garden, zoo and a statue by Rodin of Claude Lorrain (or Claude Gellée) artist.

Interestingly enough, Stanislas's idea worked out rather differently to what he had intended. Today the main square is called the Place Stanislas, and a statue to Stanislas the Magnificent stands in the centre. He is buried in the church, Notre-Dame de Bon Secours, built by Héré in 1738 in the place of a chapel constructed by René II to commemorate his victory over Charles the Rash and the Burgundians. Inside you will find the tomb of Stanislas, a sculptuary of the heart of his daughter, Marie Leczinska and the mausoleum of his wife Catherine Opalinska.

Apart from walking through its gracious, ornamented squares, the Lorraine museum, situated in the old ducal palace, and which shows the history of the region, is worth a visit, as is the Museum of Fine Arts (chiefly European painting from the 14th century onwards), situated in one of the pavilions in Place Stanislas.

The church of the Cordeliers (deconsecrated), not far from the old ducal palace, might be called the St Denis of the Dukes of Lorraine. The tombs of all the dukes are here. The Nancy School museum gives an interesting presentation of furniture design, glasswork and ceramics, pioneered by Nancy craftsmen. There is also a zoological museum (tropical aquarium and botanical garden) in rue St Cathérine.

Nancy is well-served by restaurants: the town has a famous vegetable market.

Guided evening tours of Nancy take place (floodlit old buildings add an extra dimension) mid-July to mid-September.

Nancy, on the main road between Paris and Strasbourg, makes quite a good excursion centre.

Lunch, dinner and overnight at Nancy.

Detour

Vittel

From Epinal, D166/28/3/28 to Vittel, a famous spa and resort, situated in an attractive wooded area. Its cold water springs were familiar to the Romans but they fell into disuse and were forgotten and were only much later rediscovered.

Since 1854, it has been renowned for its treatment of liver and kidney complaints, gout and rheumatism, also just for rest and relaxation. Many athletes come here to recuperate. It has a casino and extensive sporting facilities. Vittel bottled water is now more popular in France than Perrier.

Contrexéville nearby, is another spa, famous for its bottled mineral water. It too has a casino but it is a smaller town than Vittel.

On to Nancy via D429/413/913.

VITTEL: USEFUL INFORMATION	
Tourist Office:	av. Bouloumié
	Tel: (29) 08 42 03
Population:	6,440
Facilities:	Casino, spa, golf course

Hôtel d'Angleterre 🥂
Rue de Charmy
88800 Vittel
Tel: (29) 08 08 42

Built in the grand tradition of spa hotels, only five minutes from the springs themselves. Lunch in the pleasant, grassy, tree-lined garden.

Closed:	Open all year
Rooms:	62
Credit cards:	Am.Ex, Diners, Visa, Carte Bleu
Food:	Straightforward menus at reasonable prices
Rating:	★★★

NANCY: USEFUL INFORMATION

Tourist Office:	14 Place Stanislas
	Tel: (83) 35 22 41
Population:	99,307
Facilities:	Golf course (17 km), airport
Interest:	Museums, aquarium, churches

Grand Hôtel de la Reine
2 Place Stanislas
54000 Nancy
Tel: (83) 35 03 01

Set in the centre of the town this hotel offers a high standard of comfort together with exciting dishes in its restaurant. It is a member of the Relais and Châteaux group, so you can expect true luxury and quality.

Closed:	Open all year
Rooms:	51
Credit cards:	Diners, Visa, Carte Bleu, Euro
Food:	Try Blinis de Sarrasin et truffes de meuse and Mille-Feuille de crepes croquant aux fruits rouges
Rating:	★★★★

For more modest alternatives

Hôtel la Cigogne
4 bis Rue des Ponts
54000 Nancy
Tel: (83) 32 89 33

Closed:	Open all year
Rooms:	44
Facilities:	Lift, telephones in rooms
Credit cards:	Am.Ex, Diners, Visa, Euro
Food:	No restaurant, try one of the town's many alternatives
Rating:	★★★

Hôtel Crystal
5 Place Maginot
54000 Nancy
Tel: (83) 35 41 55

Closed:	Open all year
Rooms:	57
Facilities:	Television, minibars in rooms
Credit cards:	Am.Ex, Diners, Visa
Food:	No restaurant
Rating:	★★★

Meat lovers should make a point of visiting this restaurant which, as its name suggests, specializes in meat dishes.

Restaurant des Nouveaux Abattoirs
4 Boulevard d'Austrasie
54000 Nancy
Tel: (83) 35 46 25

Closed:	Saturdays and Sundays
Credit cards:	Carte Bleu, Euro
Food:	Tête de Veau, Pied de Porc, Andouillette Gras Double, Steak Poivre and Steak Tartare are a few of their specialities.
Rating:	★★

La Gentilhommière
29 rue Maréchaux
Nancy
Tel: (83) 32 26 44

Very good food which can be eaten outside.

Closed:	13 August to 4 September
Credit cards:	Euro, Visa
Rating:	★★★

La Petite Marmite
8 rue Gambetta
Nancy
Tel: (83) 35 25 63

Closed:	Saturday evenings, Sundays
Rating:	★★

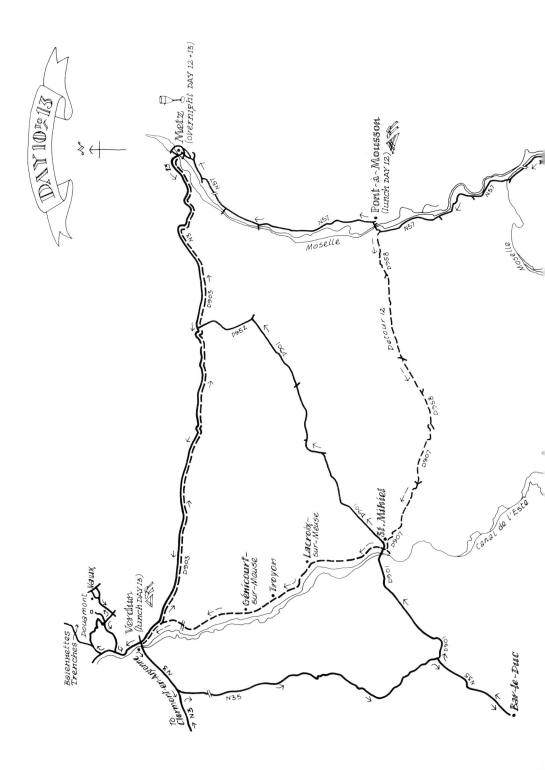

DAY 10 to 13

N

Metz (overnight DAY 12 + 13)

Pont-à-Mousson (lunch DAY 12)

Moselle

Détour 12

D958

N57

N57

N57

Moselle

D903

D952

D964

D907

D958

St. Mihiel

Lacroix-sur-Meuse

D907

Génicourt-sur-Meuse

Troyon

D964

D901

Canal de l'Este

D903

Verdun (lunch DAY 13)

Baïennettes Trenches

Douamont

Vaux

Clermont-en-Argonne

N3

N35

D990

N3

Bar-le-Duc

N35

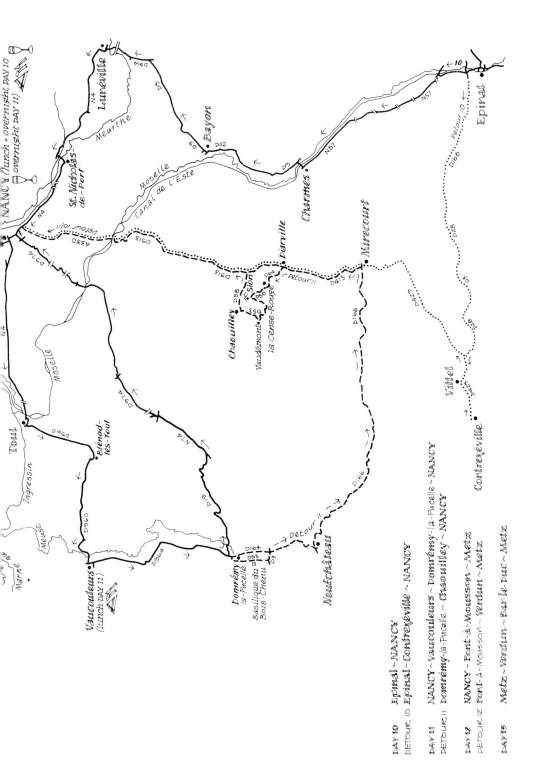

DAY 10   Epinal ~ NANCY
DETOUR 10 Epinal ~ Contrexéville ~ NANCY

DAY 11   NANCY ~ Vaucouleurs ~ Domrémy-la-Pucelle ~ NANCY
DETOUR 11 Domrémy-la-Pucelle ~ Chaouilley ~ NANCY

DAY 12   NANCY - Pont-à-Mousson ~ Metz
DETOUR 12 Pont-à-Mousson ~ Verdun ~ Metz

DAY 13   Metz ~ Verdun ~ Bar-le-Duc ~ Metz

Mirecourt

DAY 11

Nancy, Toul, Vaucouleurs, Domrémy-la-Pucelle, Nancy: approx. 107 km (67 miles)

A round trip from Nancy will encompass the region made famous by Jeanne d'Arc. After a morning in the ancient bishopric of Toul, lunch is at Vaucouleurs from where Jeanne d'Arc set off with her army to free France. A short drive south lies the village of Domrémy-la-Pucelle, where the Maid was born and the voices that inspired her were heard. In returning to Nancy you could detour via Sion-Vaudémont — scene of numerous national pilgrimages and symbol of French freedom.

Overnight at Nancy.

Map references

Nancy	6°10'E 48°42'N
Toul	5°53'E 48°41'N
Blenod-lès-Toul	5°50'E 48°36'N
Vaucouleurs	5°40'E 48°36'N
Domrémy-la-Pucelle	5°41'E 48°27'N

Detour

Neufchâteau	5°42'E 48°22'N
Sion-Vaudémont	6°05'E 48°25'N
Mirecourt	6°08'E 48°18'N
Diarville	6°08'E 48°24'N
La Cense Rouge	6°06'E 48°26'N

Route shown pp. 108-9.

Breakfast at Nancy.

N4 to Toul.

Toul

Toul is situated between the Moselle and the Canal de la Marne au Rhin. Surrounded by 18th-century ramparts (constructed by Vauban), it has four main gates. Approached from Nancy, you enter it by Porte Moselle.

Known as Tullum and the capital of the Leuci tribe, it gained importance under Roman rule. It became a Bishopric in the 10th century. When linked with Verdun and Metz, their domains formed the Trois Evêches (3 Bishoprics) territory. Toul was known as the 'striking' town because it contained 20 churches and 100 bells. Toul placed itself under French protection in 1545, lost its Bishopric in the 18th century, but then became an important garrison town. Its fortifications were considerably strengthened after the Franco-Prussian war. As a large part of the town was destroyed by fire in the last war, much of what you will see has been rebuilt and is new, but a few of the older buildings remain and are well worth seeing.

Toul's old cathedral, St Etienne (construction started at the beginning of the 13th century), with its delicately-carved facade and two 66-metres' octagonal towers, is a masterpiece of ogival flamboyant style. To note inside are its choir and 13th- and 14th-century cloisters.

You will find some of the old houses if you stroll round the town. In rue du Général-Géngoult: Nos 26, 28 and 30 are Renaissance, No. 8 is 14th century, Nos. 6, 6Bis and Hôtel de Pimodan are 17th century. In rue Gouvion St-Cyr stands the Maison Dieu (traditionally founded by Bishop St-Gerard in the 10th century, now houses the municipal museum), and Gothic and Renaissance facades and entrances at nos. 1, 18, 24, 25, 29 and 30. The Town Hall, situated at No. 10 rue de Rigny, used to be the former Bishop's Palace, but was partially destroyed in 1940. Note the Jeanne d'Arc memorial.

Take the D960 to Blenod-lès-Toul. It is worth stopping to see the early 16th-century church with its magnificent tomb of Hugues des Hazards, born locally, a famous humanist and patron of the arts who eventually became bishop of Toul.

Drive to Vaucouleurs (D960), prettily situated beside the Meuse.

Lunch at Vaucouleurs.

Jeanne d'Arc country

The Jeanne d'Arc country is situated in the Meuse valley, between Void and Neufchâteau, once a stronghold dominating the region, which often acted as a place of refuge for the people from the surrounding area.

Jeanne was 16 when she first informed the local seigneur at Vaucouleurs of the voices she had heard in the Bois-Chenu, telling her that it was she who would save France. After much persuasion and more than one visit to him, he finally provided her with an escort to go to Chinon, where she met the Dauphin Charles, the legitimate, if still uncrowned, King of France.

You can still see the ruins of the castle at Vaucouleurs where Jeanne was received by Robert de Baudricourt, the chapel where she prayed and the Porte de France, through which she rode in 1429, dressed in page's clothing, with her troops to meet the Dauphin.

Drive south to Domrémy-la-Pucelle (Domrémy the Maid) (D964), 19 kms, Lorraine's most famous village.

Domrémy-la-Pucelle

This is where Jeanne d'Arc was born. At that time Domrémy was only just in France, then largely an unborn nation. People's allegiance was mainly to their feudal lord, a local matter, for patriotism to one's country was not yet an important issue. Jeanne grew up during a period of anarchy and civil war. Bands of wandering soldiers looted houses; fields were left untilled. Probably most peasants lived wretched and insecure lives.

Jeanne was only 13 when she heard the voices of Ste Catherine and Ste Marguerite, calling her in the little garden beyond her bedroom window in the small stone cottage. She heard them calling again when walking in the nearby Bois-Chenu and, she believed, the voice of Archangel Michael as well. There had been a prophecy by Merlin that France would be saved by a woman. This may well have influenced the susceptible young girl.

Jeanne's home, near the church at Domrémy, and the village itself, were and still are typical of Lorraine. Her house can be visited; next door to it is a museum devoted to her history. Although the church has been considerably altered since her time, the medieval font in which she was baptised is still there. Her story is told in the small stained-glass windows. The Basilica du Bois-Chenu, near Domrémy, was built at the end of the last century and was consecrated in 1926. It was intended both to honour her memory and be a place of prayer for soldiers who died on the battlefield, fighting for France.

In Jeanne's day, country folk believed in fairies, invited them to baptisms and often laid an extra place for them at meals. The Bois-Chenu may once have been an ancient sacred wood, used for pagan rites. Judges sentencing Jeanne at Rouen, trying to convict her of witchcraft, suggested she met fairy ladies there.

There is an interesting theory put forward by some historians that Jeanne d'Arc was the natural daughter of Isabella of Bavaria, Queen and mother of Charles VII, and Louis Duke of Orleans, and that she had been secretly adopted by the Arc couple at Domrémy. If this were so then the King she had crowned at Rheims would have been her half brother. If it had been known to people in high places it might possibly explain the ease, comparatively speaking, with which she was able to gain support from the important people who helped her.

Return to Nancy (D19/74/974).

Dinner and overnight at Nancy.

Detour

D164 from Domrémy to Neufchâteau (about 12 kms) or D53, D3 and D164 to Neufchâteau as you will then pass the Basilica.

Neufchâteau, a small industrial town and not very interesting, lies at the crossroads of important routes. During the Middle Ages its ownership was hotly disputed by the Dukes of Champagne and Lorraine.

Not far from the town is an isolated ridge, the Colline Inspirée, the celebrated old hill of Sion-Vaudémont to which important pilgrimages are still made each

114

year. It has always been a place of prayer. The Celtic worship of the gods of war and peace was replaced by that of the Virgin Mary. Prayers were said here for the Crusades in the Holy Land. Later, under the banner of Notre-Dame de Sion, Duke René defeated Charles the Rash before Nancy.

Because it lies just inside the part of Lorraine not annexed by the Prussians in 1871, it has become a symbol of Freedom and a focus for French nationalism, almost religious in the strength of feeling it engenders.

The church here has been the scene of major national pilgrimages — in 1873, 1920, 1946 and 1973. The last one, which included war-wounded soldiers and ex-prisoners of war, was dedicated to reconciliation with Germany.

The writer, Maurice Barrés, gave this crescent-shaped ridge the name 'Colline Inspirée'. A 22 metres' monument, signifying the lantern of death, was raised to his memory in 1928 on the summit of the Signal de Vaudémont (541 metres) about 3 kms away.

To visit Sion-Vaudémont return to Nancy via Mirecourt (D166), then Diarville (D413/913), then D64, passing La Cense Rouge and then D50/50e. After viewing the church and ridge, take D53 to Chaouilley, then D58/913 to Nancy.

TOUL: USEFUL INFORMATION

Tourist Office:	parvis Cathédrale
	Tel: (83) 64 11 69
Population:	17,752
Interest:	Cathedral and church

VAUCOULEURS: USEFUL INFORMATION

Tourist Office:	23 Rue Jeanne d'Arc
	Tel: (29) 89 42 23
Population:	2,511

La Belle Epoque
31 Avenue Victor Hugo
54200 Toul
Tel: (83) 43 23 71

Closed:	2 weeks in February and Saturday and Sunday lunch-times in August
Credit cards:	Visa, Carte Bleu, Euro
Food:	Fish, foie gras
Rating:	★★

Le Relais de la Poste
12 Avenue Maginot
55140 Vaucouleurs
Tel: (29) 89 40 01

An old coaching house which serves elegant, good food. Typical dishes are terrine of three fish and Jambonneau confit.

Closed:	20 December-20 January, Sunday evenings and Mondays
Rooms:	10
Credit cards:	Mastercard, Visa, Carte Bleu, Euro
Food:	Interesting and stylish
Rating:	★★★

DAY 12

Nancy, Pont-à-Mousson, Metz: approx. 55 km (34 miles)

Leaving Nancy the tour heads north along the Moselle valley, via Pont-à-Mousson for lunch, to Metz — the city of churches where two rivers meet. From Pont-à-Mousson it is possible to detour through some of the poignant battlefields around Verdun.

Overnight at Metz.

Map references
Nancy   6°10′E 48°42′N
Pont-à-Mousson   6°04′E 48°54′N
Metz   6°10′E 49°07′N

Detour
St Mihiel   5°53′E 48°54′N
Lacroix   5°31′E 48°58′N
Troyon   5°28′E 49°00′N
Génicourt   5°26′E 49°02′N
Verdun   5°24′E 49°09′N

Route shown p. 108-9.

Breakfast at Nancy.

N57 or autoroute to Pont-à-Mousson.

Pont-à-Mousson

This old town owes its name to the 9th-century bridge spanning the Moselle. Although now mainly an industrial town, it still has a few old buildings. Place Duroc is surrounded by narrow shuttered 16th-century houses above arcaded shops. The fountain in the centre, which suffered damage in both World Wars, was a gift to the town by the Americans.

Pont-à-Mousson once possessed a University, which was founded by Charles III, Duke of Lorraine, in 1572. He wanted to train priests who could stand up to the arguments of Luther and Calvin and the reformed faith. Mary, Queen of Scots, requested that it be a seminary for Scottish priests. However, pestilence and famine forced its closure during the Thirty Years' War, and it was later transferred to Nancy in 1768. The 16th- and 17th-century buildings are now a secondary school.

Of chief interest now is the 18th-century Town Hall, 14th- to 17th-century St Martin and the 18th-century Abbey of the Prémontrés, now used as a cultural centre. The rounded Butte Mousson (7 kms away on N57), surmounted by a ruined feudal castle (also a modern church), belonging to the Counts of Barr, was the site of many battles, including those of the last war. From it is a splendid view of the province.

Lunch at Pont-à-Mousson.

From Pont-à-Mousson take the N57 to Metz for the afternoon.

Metz

Metz is pronounced 'Mess'. Drivers might agree that this is an appropriate name when making their way through its many narrow, one-way streets.

As this extremely lively city attracts businessmen as well as tourists, its hotels get booked up quickly. Make your room reservations in Metz early.

Metz, strategically situated, with a port on the canalised Moselle, is a railway junction and the centre of a complex road network. Considerably older than Nancy, it was once known as Dividorum (townlet of the gods), when it was capital of the Mediomatrices, a Gallic tribe. The Gallo-Romans called it Metti. Strongly fortified, it was a vital link in the Roman chain of command and a necessary bulwark against Germanic invasions.

Metz was evangelised in the 3rd century and was the residence of Sigisbert, King of Austrasie. Charlemagne had a particular liking for the city. In 843, Metz became the capital of Lotharingie.

Metz's golden era was in the Middle Ages when it was a free town, the capital of a small republic within the Germanic Holy Roman Empire, and governed by its own nobility, an association of aristocratic families, headed by a Prince Bishop. Its decline began when these old families died out, owing to the encroachment of turbulent neighbouring lords, and the later turmoils of the Wars of Religion.

When Metz became Protestant and was in danger of persecution, Henri II of France (reigned 1547-1559), although a Catholic himself, defended it against the Hapsburg, Charles V, in 1552. The French continued to occupy the city, and after the Treaty of Munster in 1648, Metz was ceded to France, along with Toul and Verdun. By the 18th century, it was an important citadel town near France's northwest frontier. The impressive buildings in the Place d'Armes, Porte Serpenois and the Esplanade, date from this period.

During the Franco-Prussian war, French troops retreated into Metz, where they were forced to capitulate after a 54 days' siege. Many citizens emigrated, especially to North Africa. The town's fortifications were completed by the Germans: by the end of the 19th century, Metz was one of the best protected strongholds of the German empire.

Metz did not receive much damage during the First World War, but did during the second. It was occupied by the Germans and besieged for two and a half months, holding up the allied advance during 1944. As always, Metz recovered. Now much enlarged and its business part extended, it is one of France's most dynamic and go-ahead cities.

Don't miss a visit to its Gothic cathedral, St Etienne (12th-century, on the site of two others joined together). It is celebrated throughout France for the height of its nave and the beauty of its stained-glass windows: 13th-, 14th- and

16th-century. There are also more recent additions of the 19th- and 20th-centuries; contemporary artists such as Marc Chagall and Jacques Villon were used. Its Mutte tower, 88 metres high and worth climbing for its view over the town, contains a famous bell, cast in 1605, which is rung on historic occasions.

Metz has many outstanding churches. Of particular interest are St Pierre aux Nonnains, standing on the foundations of a 4th-century basilica, claimed to be the oldest church in France; Ste Thérèse, built 1954, with a very tall, needle-like spire; and the Templar's Chapel. Metz's three main museums, Fine Arts, Gallo-Roman archaeology and Natural History, are situated in a former Carmelite convent, near the cathedral on rue du Haut-Poirier. The museum has some particularly interesting items drawn from Metz's long history (note: the remains of a Gallo-Roman thermal bath and a fine collection of medieval ceilings painted on wood).

At the end of August and beginning of September Metz holds the Mirabelle Festival (celebrating the fruit which grows locally), it includes the Grand Parade led by the Mirabelle Queen.

Metz lies in a valley where the waters of the Moselle are swollen by those of the Seille, which split up into arms as they flow through the city. Pleasant promenades are to be found on the Esplanade, Boulevard Poincaré and beside the Lac des Cygnes, also on river banks in other parts of the city.

Detour

From Pont-à-Mousson it is possible to drive across to the First World War battlefields surrounding Verdun, and into Metz for the evening. This allows little time for stopping to visit the sites and, if your schedule allows, I would recommend you make a full day trip from Metz.

For the short tour, from Pont-à-Mousson take the D958/907 to St Mihiel, then drive to Verdun beside the Meuse, a scenic route. Take the D964 past forests and Lacroix, Troyon and Génicourt then across Canal de l'Est and across the A4 follow the D34 to Verdun. From Verdun take the D903 into Metz. For details of the places visited along this route, see pp. 126-7.

Dinner and overnight at Metz.

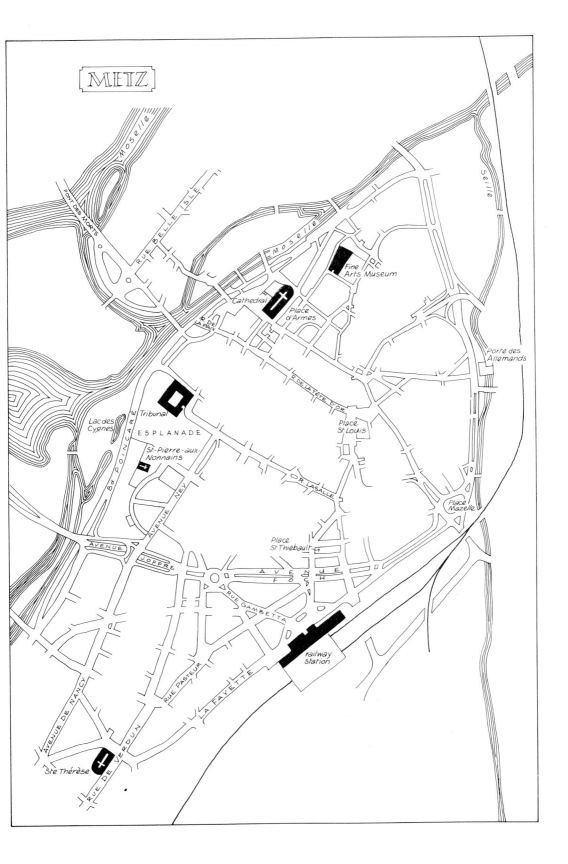

METZ

Moselle

PONT DES MORTS

RUE BELLE ISLE

Moselle

R. DE LA PAIX

Cathedral

Place d'Armes

Fine Arts Museum

Serre

Porte des Allemands

R. DE LA TÊTE D'OR

Tribunal

Lac des Cygnes

ESPLANADE

St-Pierre-aux-Nonnains

Place St. Louis

R. LASALLE

Place Mazelle

Bd POINCARÉ

AVENUE NEY

Place St. Thiébault

AVENUE

JOFFRE

AVENUE FOCH

RUE GAMBETTA

railway station

RUE PASTEUR

AVENUE DE NANCY

RUE DE VERDUN

LA FAYETTE

Ste Thérèse

Hôtel Bagatelle
49 Rue Gambetta
Pont-à-Mousson
Tel: (83) 81 03 64

This is a small hotel but the restaurant is highly recommended.

Closed:	Open all year
Rating:	★★★

Café Horne
37 Place Duroc
Pont-à-Mousson
Tel: (83) 81 04 50

Closed:	Monday, Tuesday and Wednesday evenings
Credit cards:	Am.Ex, Visa, Euro
Food:	Good value and quality with interesting wine list
Rating:	★★

Hôtel Cecil
14 Rue Pasteur
57000 Metz
Tel: (87) 66 66 13

A grand town house has been converted inside to a modern and comfortable hotel.

Closed:	Open all year
Rooms:	39
Credit cards:	Carte Bleu
Food:	No restaurant
Rating:	★★★

Hôtel Altea St Thiébaut
29 Place St Thiébaut
57000 Metz
Tel: (87) 36 17 69

This large hotel has a restaurant, Les Quatre Saisons, which serves interesting, reasonably priced food.

Closed:	Open all year
Rooms:	112
Credit cards:	Am.Ex, Diners, Visa
Rating:	★★★★

Restaurant 'La Dinanderie'
2 Rue de Paris
57000 Metz
Tel: (87) 30 14 40

A rather spectacularly decorated dining room and an exciting menu make this a place to look out for.

Closed:	Sunday evenings and Mondays
Credit cards:	Am.Ex, Visa
Food:	Try the Symphonie de petites salades et légumes croquants aux deux foies gras, salmon, langoustines
Rating:	★★★

METZ: USEFUL INFORMATION	
Tourist Office:	Place d'Armes
	118,502
Facilities:	Golf course (14 km), airport
Interest:	Cathedral, churches, museums

123

Verdun

DAY 13

The itinerary ends in Metz and from here you can begin your homeward journey. However a detour is here outlined for a day touring Verdun and surrounds. This involves a second night at Metz before finishing your holiday.

Map references

Metz	6°10′E 49°07′N
Verdun	5°24′E 49°09′N
Vaux	5°28′E 49°13′N
Douamont	5°26′E 49°14′N
Clermont-en-Argonne	5°05′E 49°06′N
Bar-le-Duc	5°10′E 48°47′N
St Mihiel	5°33′E 48°54′N

Route shown pp. 108-9.

Breakfast in Metz.

The itinerary ends in Metz. You may wish to spend the morning completing your exploration of the city before embarking on your homeward journey. However if your schedule allows then you might take the opportunity to visit the Verdun region and spend an extra night at Metz.

Detour

Some of the First World War's most horrific combats took place around Verdun, a fortified French key town, alongside the Meuse, about 65 kms to the west of Metz (D903). One can see here many reminders of its horrendous past — a citadel, monuments and memorials — but it is now a surprisingly peaceful-looking and pleasant French town.

Since the 13th century it has been noted for its sugared almonds, 'dragées', which are offered at important family events in France, such as First Communions and Weddings.

Although celebrated in history as the place where the Carolingian Empire was divided in three (843 AD), Verdun remains better-known for its epic fight in World War One, when it withstood the powerful German attack to capture the main road to Paris. That the Germans did not pass is proudly inscribed for posterity to see on the city's crest. The price paid was enormous.

Verdun and many of its surrounding villages were almost completely destroyed. A million soldiers lost their lives. About a quarter of these now lie in the 74 cemeteries situated to the north and northeast of the city. Of the rest, so many blown-up bodies were strewn over the battlefields, that it was impossible to even tell which side they were on.

The hills around Verdun have been re-forested, you can tour them and drive along the right and left banks of the Meuse. The right bank tour (21 kms) takes in the forts of Vaux and Douamont, the Bayonet Trench (in which a battalion of French soldiers chose to be buried alive rather than surrender), and the Ossuary of Douamont (not far from the place which marked the furthest point in the German advance), a permanent memorial to the 400,000 fallen French soldiers. Inside are 46 chests of bones and skulls, each one corresponding to a sector of the battlefield. The tour of the left bank and Argonne takes longer (50 kms), but is of less interest.

Clermont-en-Argonne, N3 to the west of Verdun, is sited picturesquely on a wooded hill above the Aire valley. It was once the capital of the Count of Clermontais, dominated by a castle destroyed during the Fronde rebellion, which lay on the edge of the Argonne forest. During the First World War two batteries were installed on this hill. Ironically enough, one was commanded by French Commandant Lebrun, the other by American Lieutenant Truman. Both were later to become Presidents of their respective Republics. To see here are the Chapel of Ste Anne, 16th-century and built on the site of the old castle, and St Didier church, also 16th-century.

Returning towards Verdun, turn right along the Voie Sacrée (the sacred way of World War One) the N35 which runs from Verdun across battlefields southwards to Bar-le-Duc. It was the main channel of communication (together with the railway) for the transport of troops and supplies, and the evacuation of the wounded.

Bar-le-Duc

Bar-le-Duc today is the centre of a commercial region which still attracts a number of fairs. The town is Merovingian in origin and its age is reflected in the steep streets and picturesque houses. To see are St Pierre church, built at the top of the town, 15th-century Gothic — note the famous statue to Le Squelette (the skeleton) representing René de Chalon, Prince of Orange, and made at his widow's request, the work of Ligier Richier; also the local history and science museums.

From Bar-le-Duc head north-east (N35/D901/954/903) to St Mihiel situated on the western edge of the Regional Lorraine Park.

St Mihiel, although not particularly attractive, was once the seat of an important Bénédictine abbey, and a medieval capital. The 16th century was its heyday when it produced a famous school of artists. Ligier Richier (1500-67) was born here (his house may be seen). Two of his best known works, 'The Swooning of the Virgin' and 'The Entombment' are in the churches of St Michel and St Etienne respectively.

St Mihiel, situated between hills, occupied a key position on the Meuse in the First World War. Its early capture in the war prevented the allies from using this valley and made it difficult for them to supply Verdun.

Return to Metz (D901/952/903).

```
┌────────────────────────────────────────────────────┐
│  VERDUN: USEFUL INFORMATION                          │
│  Tourist Office:        Place Nation                 │
│                         Tel: (29) 84 18 85           │
│  and                    17 Place A-Maginot           │
│                         Tel: (29) 86 06 56           │
│  Interest:              Cathedral, buildings, war    │
│                         monuments, battlefields, war │
│                         cemeteries                   │
└────────────────────────────────────────────────────┘
```

Hostellerie Coq Hardi

8 avenue Victoire
Verdun
Tel: (29) 86 36 36

Set in the centre of the town this hotel restaurant offers very good elegant food. They also pride themselves on their wines, particularly Chardonnay and Bouzy.

Closed:	22 December to 31 January and Wednesdays
Credit cards:	Am.Ex, Euro, Visa
Food:	Dishes like Canard au vinaigre de framboises and Mirabelles flambées au caramel set the standard and style
Rating:	★★★★

Restaurant 'le Turkheim'

5 et 7 avenue Garibaldi
55100 Verdun
Tel: (29) 86 34 82

Monsieur and Madame Guy Bourtot specialise in 'choucroute' dishes and all regional food.

Rating:	★★★

L'Escale
8 avenue de Paris
55100 Verdun
Tel: (29) 86 15 03

This small hotel, bar and restaurant offers good food at sensible prices.

Rating: ★★

Crèperie de la Tour
18 rue Chaussée
55100 Verdun
Tel: (29) 86 34 74

For a lighter meal this establishment would be ideal. It mainly serves crepes, both savoury and sweet, followed by an amazing choice of ice creams. They also specialise in interesting teas, of which they have a great selection.

Rating: ★★

Obernai

Recipes
from the Region

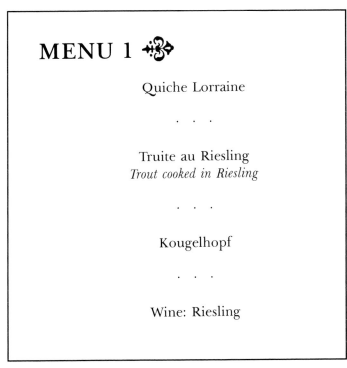

MENU 1

Quiche Lorraine

. . .

Truite au Riesling
Trout cooked in Riesling

. . .

Kougelhopf

. . .

Wine: Riesling

Quiche Lorraine

4oz/125 g smoked
bacon
1 whole egg
3 egg yolks
¼ pint/150ml crème
fraîche or double cream
4oz/125g fromage blanc
or curd cheese
salt and pepper

For the pastry
8oz/250g plain flour
salt
4oz/125g butter
1 egg
a little water

Serves 6

To make the pastry, first sift the flour and add a pinch of salt. Cut the butter into small pieces and crumble it into the flour. Break in the egg and mix with your hands. Add 3-4 tablespoons of water, as necessary, to make a soft dough. Roll it into a ball, wrap in greaseproof paper and chill for an hour. Then roll out the pastry and line a 10in/25cm flan tin. Prick the bottom with a fork.

Cut the bacon into dice and heat briefly in a frying pan so that some of the fat runs. Drain and arrange the bacon in the pastry case.

Sieve the cheese if you are using curd cheese; with fromage blanc it should not be necessary; and beat with the cream. Whisk the whole egg

133

and the egg yolks thoroughly and add to the mixture. Season with a little salt and plenty of freshly ground pepper. Pour the mixture over the bacon and bake in a preheated oven, 200°C/400°F/gas 6 for 20 minutes, then lower the temperature to 180°C/350°F/gas 4 and cook for a further 10 minutes. The filling should have puffed up and be golden brown. Serve at once.

Truite au Riesling
Trout cooked in Riesling

6 small trout
6oz/175g leeks, thinly sliced
8fl oz/150ml Riesling
1 tsp cornflour
3oz/75g butter, chilled
salt and pepper

Serves 6

Butter an ovenproof dish just large enough to hold the trout in a single layer. Spread the leeks over the bottom, season the fish and lay them on the leeks. Pour over the wine, cover the dish with buttered paper and bake in a preheated oven, 200°C/400°F/gas 6 for 10-12 minutes.

Remove the trout and leeks to a serving dish and cover. Pour the cooking liquid into a small pan, bring to the boil and reduce by half. Mix the cornflour with a little cold water and stir it into the sauce. Bring it back gently to the boil, stirring constantly. Whisk in small pieces of the chilled butter to finish the sauce. Coat the fish with the sauce and serve.

Kougelhopf

4fl oz/125ml warm milk
¼oz/10g dried yeast
3oz/75g sugar
12oz/375g strong white flour
3oz/75g raisins
1 small glass kirsch
3oz/75g butter
3 eggs
1 tbsp salt
2oz/60g split blanched almonds

Serves 6

Make a sponge with the milk, yeast, 1 teaspoon sugar and 2oz/50g flour. Set it aside to rise. Soak the raisins in the kirsch.

Beat the butter and sugar until creamy, then beat in the eggs with a tablespoon of flour. Sift the remaining flour and salt together in a mixing bowl, add the egg mixture and the yeast sponge. Fold in the flour gently at first, then beat well until you have a smooth, silky dough that rolls off the sides of the bowl. Cover the bowl with a cloth and leave to rise, about 1 hour, until doubled in volume.

Grease a 9in/23cm kougelhopf mould thoroughly with melted butter and sprinkle with the almonds.

Knock back the dough and knead for a few moments. Drain the raisins, toss them in a little flour and mix them in. Put the dough into the mould and leave to rise again for about 30 minutes, until it reaches the top of the mould. Bake in a preheated oven, 200°C/400°F/gas 6 for about 45 minutes; a skewer inserted in the kougelhopf should come out clean. Cool on a wire rack, then serve dredged with icing sugar.

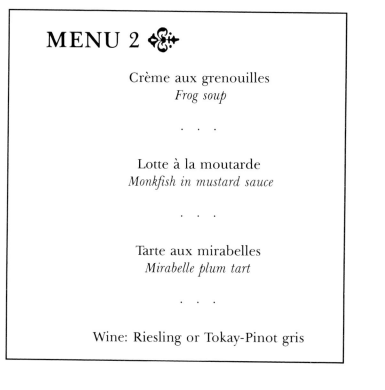

MENU 2

Crème aux grenouilles
Frog soup

. . .

Lotte à la moutarde
Monkfish in mustard sauce

. . .

Tarte aux mirabelles
Mirabelle plum tart

. . .

Wine: Riesling or Tokay-Pinot gris

Crème aux grenouilles
Frog soup

2oz/50g butter
2 shallots, finely
chopped
18 frogs' legs
4fl oz/125ml Sylvaner
2 bunches watercress
1¾ pints/1 litre chicken
stock
4 egg yolks
4fl oz/100ml cream
salt and pepper

Serves 4

Melt half the butter in a sauté pan and cook the shallots briefly, then add the frogs' legs and sauté, stirring frequently. Season with salt and pepper and add the wine. Simmer for 10 minutes, then take out the frogs' legs and leave to cool.

Clean the watercress and remove any long stalks. Heat the remaining butter and cook the watercress sprigs. Add the cooking liquor from the frogs' legs, season and bring to the boil, then sieve the watercress or put it through a vegetable mill.

Remove the bones from the frogs' legs and chop the meat. Put it in a pan with the watercress purée and the stock and heat gently. Beat the egg yolks and cream together lightly, whisk in a ladleful of stock, pour the mixture slowly into the soup, stirring all the time. Heat through gently, but do not let the soup boil.

Lotte à la moutarde
Monkfish in mustard sauce

2lb/1kg monkfish
3 shallots, chopped
4 tomatoes, peeled, seeded and cubed
¼ pint/150ml Riesling
3 tbsps Dijon mustard
1oz/25g butter
salt and pepper

For the fish fumet
2 onions, sliced
1 bay leaf
a few parsley stalks
a strip of lemon peel
1 tsp black peppercorns, crushed
1 glass Riesling
¾ pint/450ml water

Serves 4

Remove the bone and the grey, filmy skin from the monkfish and cut each fillet in two to yield four pieces of similar size.

Use the bone to make the stock. Put it in a pan with all the other ingredients for the fumet, bring to the boil and then simmer for 15 minutes. Strain the fumet and boil to reduce by two thirds.

Butter an ovenproof dish, sprinkle the shallots in it and lay the fish fillets on top. Put a spoonful of chopped tomato on each fillet. Pour the wine and the reduced fumet around the fish. Cover the dish with foil and cook in a preheated medium oven 200°C/400°F/gas 6 for 15 minutes. Lift the fish out onto a serving dish and keep warm.

Reduce the cooking liquor by half, add the

137

mustard and a knob of butter. Bring to the boil and adjust the seasoning.

Pour the sauce around the fish, spooning a little over each piece, and serve.

Tarte aux mirabelles
Mirabelle plum tart

2lb/1kg mirabelle plums
3½oz/100g sugar
ground cinnamon
icing sugar

For the pastry
see page 133

Serves 4-6

Make the pastry as described on page 133, adding two tablespoons of sugar to the flour. Line a 10in/25cm flan tin and prick the bottom with a fork. Stone the plums and cut them in 4. Arrange them in the pastry case and sprinkle with sugar. Bake in a preheated oven, 200°C/400°F/gas 6 for 25-30 minutes. Remove the tart from its tin when it is ready and sprinkle with cinnamon and icing sugar.

MENU 3 ✥

Soupe aux lentilles
Lentil soup

. . .

Baeckeoffe

. . .

Soufflé au Kirsch
Kirsch soufflé

. . .

Wine: Pinot blanc or Sylvaner

Soupe aux lentilles
Lentil soup

10oz/300g lentils, soaked in water for two hours
2 carrots
2 leeks
1 stalk celery
1 onion
2 cloves
3oz/175 butter
4oz/125g smoked bacon, diced
3 smoked pork sausages
1 bay leaf
3½ pints/2 litres water
salt and pepper

Serves 6

Chop the carrots, leeks and celery. Peel the onion and stick the cloves into it. Heat half the butter and sweat the chopped vegetables and bacon until softened. Add the drained lentils, the onion, bay leaf, water and pepper to taste. Bring to the boil then cover and cook over low heat for 1½ hours. Simmer the sausages in a pan of water for 15 minutes, then drain and slice them. Discard the bay leaf and cloves, chop the onion and return it to the pan with the sausages. Taste for seasoning and add a little salt if necessary. Stir in the remaining butter and serve very hot.

Baeckeoffe

1lb/500g shoulder of pork
1lb/500g shoulder of lamb
1lb/500g chuck or blade steak
2lb/1kg potatoes
1lb/500g onions
8oz/250g leeks
2 cloves garlic
bouquet garni
1 bottle Sylvaner
a little lard or goose fat
salt and pepper
2 pig's trotters, split in half (optional)

Serves 6

Cut the meats into equal portions and marinate for 24 hours in some of the wine with a large sliced onion, the crushed garlic, and the bouquet garni.

Slice the potatoes into rounds ¼in/5mm thick. Chop the onions and leeks. Drain the meat, reserving the marinade.

Grease an earthenware casserole with the lard or goose fat, cover the bottom with a layer of leeks and onions, then a layer of potatoes. Then put in the meat, keeping each kind separate, pork to one side, lamb in the middle, beef to the other side. Put the remaining leeks and onions and then the potatoes on the top. As you build the layers season each one with salt and pepper. Pour in the marinade liquid and the rest of the wine. Put the trotters on top.

Cover with the lid and to make sure it is tightly closed, seal it with a flour and water paste, or put a layer of foil underneath the lid. Transfer the casserole to a preheated oven, 180°C/350°F/gas 4 and cook for 2½-3 hours. Serve the baeckeoffe straight from the casserole.

Soufflé au kirsch
Kirsch soufflé

2oz/50g butter
2 tbsps flour
2 tbsps potato flour
7fl oz/200ml milk
3oz/75g sugar
4 egg yolks
5 tbsps kirsch
6 egg whites
3 sponge finger biscuits, crumbled and soaked in a little kirsch

Serves 6

Melt the butter and stir in the flour and the potato flour. Bring the milk to the boil with the sugar and pour into the flour and butter roux. Cook for about 3 minutes, stirring constantly. Remove the pan from the heat and leave to cool. Then stir in the egg yolks, one at a time and add the kirsch. Beat the egg whites until very stiff and carefully fold them into the mixture with a spatula.

Butter and dust with caster sugar a 9in/23cm soufflé dish. Pour in half of the soufflé mixture, sprinkle a layer of the sponge finger biscuits over it, then add the remaining soufflé mixture. The dish should be about ¾ full.

Bake in a preheated oven, 200°C/400°F/gas 6 for 25-30 minutes. Sprinkle with icing sugar and serve at once.

MENU 4

Cervelas en salade
Cervelas salad

. . .

Poulet à la bière
Chicken in beer

. . .

Tarte au fromage blanc
Cream cheese tart

. . .

Wine: Pinot blanc, or drink Alsace beer

Cervelas en salade
Cervelas salad

4 cervelas sausages
4 medium tomatoes
2 hard boiled eggs
6-8 lettuce leaves
1 small onion, chopped finely
2 tbsps chopped parsley
2 tbsps wine vinegar
4 tbsps olive oil
1 tsp Dijon mustard
salt and pepper

Serves 4

Skin the sausages, cut them in half lengthways and make 2 or 3 diagonal cuts across the rounded side. Cut the tomatoes in quarters and the eggs in half.

Shred or tear the lettuce leaves and spread them on a serving dish. Arrange the cervelas in the centre surrounded by the tomatoes. Sprinkle the chopped onion and parsley over the sausages. Make a vinaigrette with the vinegar, oil, mustard, salt and pepper. Spoon it over the salad and serve.

Poulet à la bière
Chicken in beer

2oz/50g butter
1 chicken weighing 3-
4lb/1.5-2kg
2 shallots, chopped
½ pint/300ml Alsace
beer
a small glass of marc or
brandy
6oz/175g small
mushrooms, sliced
2fl oz/50ml double
cream
salt and black pepper

Serves 4

Melt the butter in a large casserole, put in the chicken, seasoned with salt and pepper, and turning and basting frequently, brown it on all sides. Put in the chicken on one side and put the casserole into a preheated oven, 240°C/475°F/ gas 9 for 15 to 20 minutes, then turn the chicken to the other side and return to the oven for a further 15-20 minutes.

Take the casserole from the oven, lift out the chicken and cook the shallots briefly in the butter remaining in the casserole. Put back the chicken, breastbone up, add the beer, marc and mushrooms and return the dish to the oven for 15 minutes.

When the chicken is cooked remove it from the casserole, cut it into 4 and keep warm on a serving dish. Boil the cooking liquid to reduce it by half, stir in the cream and pour the sauce over the chicken. Serve at once with fresh noodles.

Tarte au fromage blanc
Cream cheese tart

1lb/500g cream cheese
6fl oz/175ml crème
fraîche or double cream
2 whole eggs
2 egg yolks
6oz/175g caster sugar
1 tbsp flour
vanilla extract

For the pastry
see page 133

Serves 4-6

Make the pastry as described on page 133, adding 2 tablespoons sugar to the flour. Line a 10in/25cm flan tin and prick the bottom with a fork.

Sieve the cream cheese and beat in the cream, then the eggs and the egg yolks, one at a time. Stir in the sugar mixed with the flour, and add a few drops of vanilla extract. Pour the filling into the pastry case and bake in a preheated oven, 220°C/425°F/gas 7 for another 20 minutes, then lower to 180°C/350°F/gas 4 and bake for another 20 minutes. Serve hot or cold, sprinkled with icing sugar.

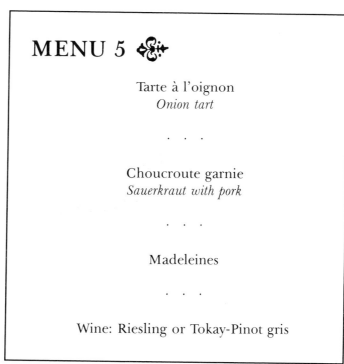

MENU 5

Tarte à l'oignon
Onion tart

. . .

Choucroute garnie
Sauerkraut with pork

. . .

Madeleines

. . .

Wine: Riesling or Tokay-Pinot gris

Tarte à l'oignon
Onion tart

1lb/500g onions
4oz/125g butter
1 tbsp oil
1 tbsp flour
8fl oz/250ml milk
8fl oz/250ml crème
fraîche or double cream
4 eggs
salt, pepper and ground
mace

For the pastry
see page 133

Serves 6

Chop the onions and cook them very slowly for about 20 minutes in the butter and oil until softened but still pale in colour. Sprinkle them with the flour, stir well and cook briefly. Remove the pan from the heat and add the milk and cream. Season with salt, pepper and ground mace, then add the well beaten eggs.

Line a loose bottomed flan tin with the pastry, pour in the onion mixture and bake in a preheated oven, 180°C/350°F/gas 4 for about 30 minutes, or until the egg and cream mixture is just set.

Remove the tart from the tin and serve.

145

Choucroute garnie
Sauerkraut with pork

4lb/2kg sauerkraut
2 onions
4oz/125g lard
2lb/1kg uncooked
smoked loin or
shoulder of pork
10oz/300g smoked
bacon in a piece
10oz/300g salt pork
1 bay leaf
6 juniper berries
3 cloves, crushed
3 cloves garlic
¾ pint/450ml Sylvaner
or Pinot Blanc
6 smoked pork sausages
salt and pepper

Serves 6-8

If any of the meats are very salty, soak for an hour in cold water. Drain the sauerkraut and if it is too salty wash in cold water.

Chop the onions, melt the lard in a large casserole and sweat the onion for a few minutes. Put in the smoked loin, smoked bacon and salt pork, cover with the sauerkraut and add the bay leaf, spices and garlic. Pour over the wine and add a little water if necessary — the sauerkraut should be almost covered. Cover the casserole tightly and cook in preheated oven, 180°C/350°F/gas 4, for 2 hours.

Towards the end of the cooking time poach the sausages in barely simmering water for 10 minutes.

Remove the meats from the casserole, slice them and keep warm. Pile the sauerkraut in the centre of a warmed serving platter and arrange the meats and sausages around and over it. Serve boiled potatoes separately and make sure there is a pot of mustard on the table.

Madeleines

5 eggs
8oz/250g caster sugar
8oz/250g plain flour,
sifted
1 tsp baking powder
salt
grated rind of 2 lemons
8oz/250g butter, melted

(Makes 24 cakes)

Madeleines are baked in special moulds that are fluted rather like a scallop shell. If you don't have any they can be baked in small bun tins. Butter and flour the moulds before making the cakes.

Beat the eggs and sugar together until rich and creamy. Add the flour, baking powder, salt and lemon rind and mix well. Pour in the melted butter and stir until blended.

Half fill the moulds and leave to stand for 10 minutes, then bake in a preheated oven, 220°C/425°F/gas 7, until risen and golden, 12-15 minutes. Remove the trays from the oven and cool the madeleines on a wire rack.

Wissembourg

Glossary of Food Terms

Starters

charcuterie	cold meats (pork)
crudités	raw vegetables
escargots	snails
potage	soup
terrine	a type of coarse pâté

Meats (Viande)

agneau (gigot de)	lamb (leg of)
andouillette	chitterling sausages
backeoffe	mixed meats and root vegetable casserole
boeuf (filet de)	beef (fillet steak)
bleu	very rare
saignant	rare
à point	medium
bien cuit	well done
brochette	kebab
côte/côtelette	chop
entrecôte	steak (rib)
jambon	ham
jarret (de veau)	knuckle (of veal)
lapin	rabbit
lièvre	hare
mouton	mutton
rillettes	potted pork
saucisse	sausage (fresh)
saucisson	sausage (dry)
tourte	pork and veal pie
veau	veal

Offal (Abats)

boudin	black pudding
cervelle	brains
foie	liver
langue	tongue
ris	sweetbreads
rognon	kidney

Poultry (Volaille) and Game (Gibier)

caille	quail
canard/caneton	duck/duckling
coq	cockerel
faisan	pheasant
oie	goose
perdrix	partridge
pintade	guinea fowl
poulet	chicken
sanglier	wild boar

Fish (Poisson) and Shellfish (Crustacés/Coquillages)

alose	shad
anguilles (en gelée)	eels (jellied)
bouquet	prawn
brochet	pike
cabillaud	cod
coquilles St. Jacques	scallops
crevettes	prawns/shrimps
écrevisse	crayfish
fruits de mer	mixed shellfish
hareng	herring
homard	lobster
huitres	oysters
langoustine	scampi
lamproie	lamprey
lotte	monkfish
loup de mer	sea bass
maquereau	mackerel
matelot	fish stew
moules	mussels
plié	plaice
pochouse	freshwater fish stew
rascasse	fish soup
sandre	perch
saumon	salmon
truite	trout

Vegetables (Léumes)

ail	garlic
artichaut	artichoke (globe)
asperge	asparagus
bettes	swiss chard

carotte	carrot
champignon	mushroom
chou	cabbage
choucroute	sauerkraut
choufleur	cauliflower
épinards	spinach
girolles	chanterelle mushrooms
haricots verts	French beans
knepfle	semolina/potato dumplings
morilles	mushrooms
mousserons	mushrooms
navet	turnip
oignon	onion
petits pois	peas
pleurotes	mushrooms
poireau	leek
poivron	green/red pepper
pomme de terre	potato
au four	baked, roast
purée	mashed
riz	rice
sarments	vine shoots

Fruit

agrumes	citrus fruit
ananas	pineapples
cassis	blackcurrant
cerise	cherry
citron	lemon
fraise	strawberry
framboise	raspberry
groseille	redcurrant
mûr	blackberry
pamplemousse	grapefruit
pêche	peach
poire	pear
pomme	apple
prune	plum

Further Reading

True Story of the Maid of Orleans Maurice David-Darnac, trs. Peter de Polnay, W.H. Allen, 1969
In the Steps of Joan of Arc Leighton Houghton, Rich and Cowan, 1951
Sisters, Alsace Lorraine by Bernard Newman, Herbert Jenkins, 1950
Vosges, Lorraine-Alsace, Green Michelin Guide (French)

Geographical Index

Aire, valley 127
Augsberg 20

Ballon d'Alsace 94
Bar-le-Duc 30, 125, 127
Bayon 99, 100
Blanc, lake 85, 86-7
Blenod-lès-Toul 111, 112
Bois-Chenu 113, 114
Bonhomme, Col du 85, 86, 87
—, Le 85, 87, 88
Bouxwiller 53, 55
Bruche, river 48, 61, 64
Bruyères 21

Calvaire, Col de 85, 86
Cense Rouge, La 111, 115
Cernay 75, 79, 91, 94
Champ du Feu 69
Chaouilley 111, 115
Charmes-sur-Moselle 19, 99, 100
Châtenois 69, 70
Clermont-en-Argonne 125
Colmar 7, 13, 16, 20, 24, 40, 64, 75,
    77-81, 85, 86
Colombey-les-Deux-Eglises 16
Contrexéville 7, 14, 30, 99, 104
Crêtes, Route des (Crest Road) 7, 86, 93-4
Cuves, Saut des 85, 87

Dabo 59, 60, 61-2
Diarville 111, 115
Dieuze 14, 19
Doller 94
Domrémy-la-Pucelle 111, 113
Donon 60
Douamont 125, 126

Epinal 91, 93, 95-7, 100, 104

Falkenstein, castle 48, 54
Fecht, valley 86
Fleckenstein, castle 48, 53, 54
Fraize 85, 87

Gazon du Fang 85, 86
Génicourt 117, 120
Gérardmer 7, 85, 87-9, 91, 92, 93
Giessen, valley 70
Girsberg 72
Grand Ballon 91, 94
Grossman 60
Grossthal, valley 60

Haguenau 16, 47, 48-9, 50-1
Haselbourg 59, 60
Haut Barr 55
Haut Griffon 55
Haut-Koenigsbourg, castle 69, 70-1
Haut Ribeaupierre 72
Hohneck, Le 85, 86, 93
Hohwald, Le 69, 70, 74
Hunawihr 76
Hunspach 47, 49

Ill, river 40
Ingwiller 53, 55

Joffre, Route 94

Kaysersberg 16, 19, 75, 76-7
Kintzheim 18

Lacroix 117, 118
Landau 16
Lapoutroie 85, 87
Lauter, river 47, 49
Lembach 53, 54
Louiz-Arzviller, canal 60
Lunéville 21, 99, 100

153

Index of Recipes

Hors d'Oeuvres

Main Courses

Puddings